my revision notes

OCR AS History
DICTATORSHIP AND DEMOCRACY IN GERMANY
1933–63

Nicholas Fellows

Series editors:
Robin Bunce and
Laura Gallagher

HODDER
EDUCATION
AN HACHETTE UK COMPANY

The Publishers would like to thank the following for permission to reproduce copyright material:
Photo credits
p.66 © Photos 12/Alamy

Orders: please contact Bookpoint Ltd, 130 Milton Park, Abingdon, Oxon OX14 4SB.
Telephone: +44 (0)1235 827720. Fax: +44 (0)1235 400454. Lines are open 9.00a.m.–5.00p.m.,
Monday to Saturday, with a 24-hour message answering service. Visit our website at
www.hoddereducation.co.uk.

© Nicholas Fellows 2012
First published in 2012 by
Hodder Education,
an Hachette UK company
338 Euston Road
London NW1 3BH

Impression number   10 9 8 7 6 5 4 3
Year   2016 2015 2014

Cover photo © chriszwaenepoel – Fotolia

Typeset in 11/13pt Stempel Schneidler by Pantek Media, Maidstone, Kent
Artwork by Pantek Media
Printed and bound in Dubai

A catalogue record for this title is available from the British Library

ISBN 978 1 444 15222 7

Contents

Introduction

About Unit F964

Unit F964 is worth 50 per cent of your AS level. It requires detailed knowledge of a period of European or world history and the ability to explore and analyse historical sources.

Overall, 64 per cent of the marks available are awarded for source analysis (Assessment Objective 2), and 36 per cent for using own knowledge to form an explanation (Assessment Objective 1).

In the exam, you are required to answer one question with two parts. Part (a) is worth 30 marks and Part (b) is worth 70 marks. The exam lasts for one hour and thirty minutes, unless you have been awarded extra time. It is advisable to spend approximately one-third of your time in the exam on Part (a) and the remaining two thirds on Part (b).

Part (a) tests your ability to:

■ comprehend source material
■ compare source material in detail, explaining how the sources agree and differ
■ suggest reasons why the sources agree or differ based on their provenance
■ reach an overall judgement.

Part (b) tests your ability to:

■ select information that focuses on the issue in the question
■ organise this information to provide an answer to the question
■ integrate information from the sources and own knowledge
■ weigh evidence from sources and own knowledge to reach an overall judgement.

Dictatorship and Democracy in Germany 1933–63

The exam board specifies that students should study four key issues as part of this topic.

1. How effectively did Hitler establish and consolidate Nazi authority 1933–45?
2. To what extent did the Nazis transform German society?
3. To what extent and in what ways did communism transform the GDR?
4. How far did Western democratic structures (political, economic and social) succeed in the Federal Republic?

How to use this book

This book has been designed to help you to develop the knowledge and skills necessary to succeed in the exam. The book is divided into four sections – one for each key issue of the course. Each section is made up of a series of topics organised into double-page spreads. On the left-hand page, you will find a summary of the key content you need to learn. Words in bold in the key content are defined in the glossary. On the right-hand page, you will find exam-focused activities. Together, these two strands of the book will take you through the knowledge and skills essential for exam success.

▼ Key historical content   ▼ Exam-focused activities

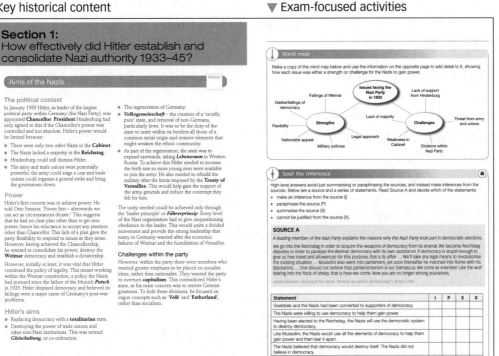

There are three levels of exam-focused activities:

- Band 1 activities are designed to develop the foundational skills needed to pass the exam. These have a turquoise heading and this symbol.

- Band 2 activities are designed to build on the skills developed in Band 1 activities and help you achieve a C grade. These have an orange heading and this symbol.

- Band 3 activities are designed to enable you to access the highest grades. These have a purple heading and this symbol.

Some of the activities have answers or suggested answers on pages 73–77 and have the following symbol to indicate this: **(a)**

Others are intended for you to complete in pairs and assess by comparing answers and these don't have answers.

Each section ends with an exam-style question and model A-grade answer with examiner's commentary. This should give you guidance on what is required to achieve the top grades.

You can also keep track of your revision by ticking off each topic heading in the book, or by ticking the checklist on the contents page. Tick each box when you have:

- revised and understood a topic
- completed the activities.

Section 1:
How effectively did Hitler establish and consolidate Nazi authority 1933–45?

The political context

In January 1933 Hitler, as leader of the largest political party within Germany (the Nazi Party), was appointed **Chancellor**. **President** Hindenburg had only agreed to this if the Chancellor's power was controlled and not absolute. Hitler's power would be limited because:

- There were only two other Nazis in the **Cabinet**.
- The Nazis lacked a majority in the **Reichstag**.
- Hindenburg could still dismiss Hitler.
- The army and trade unions were potentially powerful: the army could stage a *coup* and trade unions could organise a general strike and bring the government down.

Power

Hitler's first concern was to achieve power. He told Otto Strasser, 'Power first – afterwards we can act as circumstances dictate.' This suggests that he had no clear plan other than to get into power; hence his reluctance to accept any position other than Chancellor. This lack of a plan gave the party flexibility to respond to issues as they arose. However, having achieved the Chancellorship, he wanted to consolidate his power, destroy the **Weimar** democracy and establish a dictatorship.

However, initially at least, it was vital that Hitler continued the policy of legality. This meant working within the Weimar constitution, a policy the Nazis had pursued since the failure of the Munich *Putsch* in 1923. Hitler despised democracy and believed its failings were a major cause of Germany's post-war problems.

Hitler's aims

- Replacing democracy with a **totalitarian** state.
- Destroying the power of trade unions and other non-Nazi institutions. This was termed *Gleichschaltung*, or co-ordination.
- The regeneration of Germany.
- *Volksgemeinschaft* – the creation of a 'racially pure' state, and removal of non-Germans, particularly Jews. It was to be the duty of the state to unite within its borders all those of a common racial origin and remove elements that might weaken the ethnic community.
- As part of the regeneration, the state was to expand eastwards, taking *Lebensraum* in Western Russia. To achieve this Hitler needed to increase the birth rate so more young men were available to join the army. He also needed to rebuild the military after the limits imposed by the **Treaty of Versailles**. This would help gain the support of the army generals and reduce the contempt they felt for him.

The unity needed could be achieved only through the 'leader principle' or *Führerprinzip*. Every level of the Nazi organisation had to give unquestioning obedience to the leader. This would unite a divided movement and provide the strong leadership that many in Germany wanted after the economic failures of Weimar and the humiliation of Versailles.

Challenges within the party

However, within the party there were members who wanted greater emphasis to be placed on socialist ideas, rather than nationalist. They wanted the party to overturn **capitalism**. This contradicted Hitler's aims, as his main concern was to restore German greatness. To hide these divisions, he focused on vague concepts such as '*Volk*' and '**Fatherland**', rather than socialism.

Mind map

Make a copy of the mind map below and use the information on the opposite page to add detail to it, showing how each issue was either a strength or challenge for the Nazis to gain power.

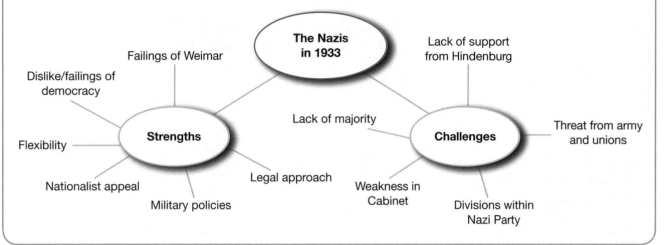

Spot the inference

High-level answers avoid just summarising or paraphrasing the sources, and instead make inferences from the sources. Below are a source and a series of statements. Read Source A and decide which of the statements:

- make an inference from the source (I)
- paraphrase the source (P)
- summarise the source (S)
- cannot be justified from the source (X).

SOURCE A

A leading member of the Nazi Party explains the reasons why the Nazi Party took part in democratic elections.

We go into the Reichstag in order to acquire the weapons of democracy from its arsenal. We become Reichstag deputies in order to paralyse the Weimar democracy with its own assistance. If democracy is stupid enough to give us free travel and allowances for this purpose, that is its affair … We'll take any legal means to revolutionise the existing situation … Mussolini also went into parliament, yet soon thereafter he marched into Rome with his Blackshirts … One should not believe that parliamentarism is our Damascus. We come as enemies! Like the wolf tearing into the flock of sheep, that is how we come. Now you are no longer among yourselves.

Joseph Goebbels, Der Angriff, The Attack, 'What do we want in the Reichstag?', 30 April 1928

Statement	I	P	S	X
Goebbels and the Nazis had been converted to supporters of democracy.				
The Nazis were willing to use democracy to help them gain power.				
Having been elected to the Reichstag, the Nazis will use the democratic system to destroy democracy.				
Like Mussolini, the Nazis would use all the elements of democracy to help them gain power and then tear it apart.				
The Nazis believed that democracy would destroy itself. The Nazis did not believe in democracy.				
Weimar democracy was strong; that is why the Nazis wanted its weapons.				
The Nazis intended to use legal means to overthrow democracy.				

Nazi admission to power in 1933

Revised

The political situation

Party	Seats in Reichstag July 1932	Seats in Reichstag November 1932
NSDAP (Nazi)	230	196
DNVP (Nationalists)	37	52
DVP (German People's Party)	7	11
Centre Party	75	70
State Party	4	2
SPD (Social Democratic Party)	133	121
KPD (Communist Party)	89	100
The Economy Party	2	1

Before Hitler was appointed Chancellor in 1933 support for the Nazis had declined from a high point in the July 1932 election (see table). Following the November election Hitler was the leader of the largest party, but had no overall majority. He refused the offer of a place in the Cabinet.

The role of political intrigue

After the election there was a period of political intrigue between the new Chancellor, von Papen, and the former Chancellor, von Schleicher.

- Von Papen was unable to get a majority, as the Nazis opposed him. He was dismissed and replaced by von Schleicher.
- Von Schleicher tried to split the Nazis by offering **Strasser** a Cabinet post.
- Von Schleicher tried to get support from the SPD. This worried industrialists and landowners, who backed a von Papen–Hitler **coalition**.

- Von Papen wanted revenge for being removed by von Schleicher, and entered into talks with the Nazis.
- Von Schleicher was unable to obtain a majority in the Reichstag.
- President Hindenburg lost confidence in the government and instructed von Papen to form a government with the Nazis.
- Von Schleicher resigned on 28 January 1933.

Hindenburg and the Nazis

Hindenburg disliked Hitler and the Nazis, but believed the party was in decline and would not be a threat. It appeared to be time for a Nationalist–Nazi coalition. Hitler demanded the position of Chancellor. Von Papen agreed, as he believed that with nine Cabinet posts for the Nationalists, and only two for the Nazis, they would be able to control Hitler. Hindenburg agreed, and Hitler became Chancellor on 30 January 1933.

Evidence the coalition could have been avoided	Evidence the coalition could not have been avoided
The Nazis only gained votes because of unemployment, which would decline as recovery started.	The army and **elites** were not strong enough to establish an authoritarian regime or achieve a majority on their own.
The Nazi Party was almost bankrupt after numerous election campaigns.	To achieve a majority, they needed Hitler.
The Nazi Party had not been able to fulfil its promises to voters, as it could not get into power.	It appeared as if Hitler's position was weak and could be controlled, so there was no need to avoid his appointment.
The economy had started to recover.	There was a belief that, once in power, Hitler would become a moderate and that would burst the Nazi bubble.

Despite apparent weaknesses (see table above), opponents had ignored Hitler's skill, charisma and determination. Within a month, events would allow him to use the powers of Weimar to overthrow the democracy.

Below is an exam-style question which asks how far you agree with a specific statement. Below this are a series of general statements which are relevant to the question. Using your own knowledge, the information on the opposite page and Sources A and B, decide which general statements support or challenge the statement in the question and tick the appropriate box.

'Hitler and the Nazi Party seized power in January 1933.' Using the sources and your own knowledge, how far do you agree with this view?

	SUPPORT	CHALLENGE
Hitler's appointment as Chancellor was the result of constitutional procedures.		
Nazi support was in decline and therefore they had to seize power.		
It was electoral support that brought Hitler to power.		
Intrigue, rather than seizure of power, best describes Hitler's appointment as Chancellor.		
Rather than seizing power, other figures believed they were using Hitler.		
The events of January 1933 have only been called a seizure of power by the press.		
It appealed to Hitler's sense of drama that the events of January 1933 were called a seizure of power.		
Hitler's dislike of democracy resulted in the events of January 1933 being called a seizure of power.		
Hitler and the Nazi Party came to power because of their electoral strength.		

SOURCE A

Hermann Goering, a leading Nazi, responding to questions at the War Trials in 1946.

Goering: At that time it was completely legal, because the National Socialist Party was then the strongest party, and the strongest party nominated the Reich Chancellor and had the greatest influence. It must not be interpreted to mean that they usurped the power, but that they had the most influential and prominent position among the parties, that is, by the completely legal means of election.

Question: You want to change the word 'seizure'?

Goering: I have to change that. It is only an expression which was common in the Press at that time.

From *Trial of Major War Criminals* Vol. 8, 1946

SOURCE B

A historian comments about the Nazis coming to power in 1933.

The Nazis used the melodramatic term 'seizure of power' to describe what was actually a complex process of bargaining and intrigue in which they were not always the main actors. The outcome was never certain, for at least once during this high stakes poker game a despondent Hitler spoke of suicide, if his party should disintegrate under the weight of frustrated expectations.

From Michael Burleigh, *The Third Reich*, 2000

Nazi consolidation of power

The Legal Revolution

Hitler created a dictatorship using legal methods:

- **27 February 1933**: Reichstag fire.
  The Parliament building in Berlin was burnt down and the Communists were blamed and banned. This was used to justify measures against Communists.
- **28 February 1933**: Decree for the Protection of the People and the State.
  As a result of the fire, Hitler was granted emergency powers.
  Political and civil liberties were suspended and many anti-Nazis were arrested.
- **5 March 1933**: Election.
  Hitler called fresh elections to the Reichstag in the hope of winning an overall majority.
  The Nazi vote increased to 43.9%. Nationalist support was still needed.
- **23 March 1933**: **Enabling Act.**
  With many members absent and others intimidated, the Reichstag voted by the necessary two-thirds majority to give Hitler total power and therefore end democracy.
  Parliamentary procedure and legislation was ended. Full power was transferred to the Chancellor and government. A dictatorship based on legality was created.
- **14 July 1933**: The Nazi Party became the only legal political party.
  Hitler used his powers to ban other political parties. Germany became a one-party state.

Co-ordination (Gleischaltung)

Gleischaltung was the Nazification of society, ensuring co-operation with the regime. It was put into practice at a local level – 'revolution from below' – by the **SA** (*Sturm Abteilung* – Stormtroopers), and at a national level – 'revolution from above' – from Berlin.

The idea was to merge German society with Nazi Party institutions and associations with the aim of allowing Nazis to control cultural, social and educational activity. However, the first concern was political, as the table at the bottom of the page shows.

Success?

In some areas the Nazis did have control. However, they did not control the Church, army or big business, and had only partial control of the civil service and education. Hitler's power was limited because he did not want to lose the support of important groups. However, he was under pressure from the SA to implement further changes.

The Night of the Long Knives

Hitler had to deal with opposition within his own party. SA chief Ernst Röhm wanted to merge the army and the SA. Army chiefs refused due to the SA's indiscipline. Hitler chose to execute Röhm and the SA leaders on 'The Night of the Long Knives' in April 1934. This had numerous consequences:

- It removed the SA and won the support of the conservative right. The army took an oath of personal loyalty to Hitler.
- The **SS** (*Shutz Staffel* – Hitler's personal guard), which had been a wing of the SA, emerged as an independent organisation.
- Hitler secured his dictatorship: he had been allowed to get away with the legal murder of opponents.

Hitler's dominance was confirmed when Hindenburg died in August 1934 and Hitler merged the role of Chancellor and President into Führer.

Institution	What happened?
Federal States	• Regional parliaments were dissolved and then abolished. • Reich governors were created. • Federal government and governors were subordinated to central government.
Political Parties	• Communists were banned after the Reichstag fire. • The Social Democrats Party was banned and their assets were seized. • Most parties agreed to dissolve themselves. • The Nazis became the only legal party.
Trade Unions	• Union premises were occupied, funds were seized and leaders were sent to concentration camps. • Independent unions were banned and replaced by the German Labour Front (**DAF**).

Explain the difference

Sources A and B give different accounts of who was to blame for the Reichstag fire. List the ways in which the sources differ. Explain the differences between the sources using the provenance of the sources alone.

SOURCE A

A historian's account based on the testimony of Karl Ernst, who was the leader of the Berlin SA. He was killed in Hitler's purge of the SA a year after the fire.

An underground passage, built to carry the central heating system, ran from Goering's palace to the Reichstag building. Through this tunnel Karl Ernst led a small detachment of Stormtroopers. They scattered gasoline and self-igniting chemicals and then made their way back to the palace.

This account was based on the testimony of Karl Ernst, the leader of the Berlin SA, who was killed in Hitler's purge of the SA a year after the fire.

William Shirer, a historian, writing in 1960; adapted from *The Rise and Fall of the Third Reich*

SOURCE B

Rudolf Hess, head of the Prussian political police, reports Hitler's immediate reaction to the fire.

'This is beginning of the Communist revolt, they will start their attack now! Not a moment must be lost!' Hitler turned to the assembled company. He shouted uncontrollably: 'There will be no mercy now. Anyone who stands in our way will be cut down. Every Communist official will be shot where he is found.'

'That is something really cunning, prepared a long time ago. The criminals have thought this out beautifully, but they've miscalculated, haven't they?'

Rudolf Hess writing in 1950

 Write the question

Sources C and D relate to the Nazi revolution and its progress by the end of 1933. Read page 8 detailing what you need to know about the Nazi consolidation of power. Having done this, write a exam-style part (a) question (see page 2) using Sources C and D.

SOURCE C

The leader of the SA makes clear his determination to continue the Nazi revolution.

A tremendous victory has been won, but not absolute victory! The SA and SS will not tolerate the German revolution going to sleep now or being betrayed at the half way stage by non-combatants. There is a fantasy in the minds of some 'co-ordinated' people, and even some who call themselves National Socialists, that to keep calm is the first duty of a citizen. This is a betrayal of the German revolution. The 'national' revolution has already lasted too long. It is high time the national revolution became the National Socialist one. Whether the middle class like it or not, we will continue our struggle.

From a speech by Ernst Röhm, leader of the SA, June 1933

SOURCE D

A complaint from a former Chancellor about the possibility of another revolution.

There appears to be endless talk of a second wave which will complete the revolution. Anyone who irresponsibly toys with such ideas should not deceive himself about the fact that a second wave can easily be followed by a third, that he who threatens the guillotine is the first to come under the knife. Nor is it clear in what direction this second wave is meant to lead. At some stage the movement must come to an end; at some point there must emerge a firm social structure held together by a legal system secure against pressure and by a State power that is unchallenged. A ceaseless dynamic creates nothing.

Von Papen, writing in 1933

Hitler and government

What was Hitler's role?

The image of the Führer was of an all-powerful dictator. He was leader of the party, and combined the roles of Chancellor, President and commander-in-chief of the armed forces. His will was law both in the party and Germany, at least in theory. He was portrayed as having the vision and will to transform Germany.

However, although Hitler had destroyed much of the opposition, there were still rival power systems which overlapped. These included the central government, with the ministries and civil service, and the SS and the Nazi Party.

As a result Hitler's role was limited:

- There was no all-embracing constitution in the Third Reich. This meant that government and law emerged in a haphazard form.
- In practice, no individual could control all areas of government.
- Hitler relied on subordinates to put his wishes into practice.
- Hitler's own personality and lifestyle involved long sleeping hours and absences from Berlin.

Hitler's day-to-day role was limited. He avoided decision-making and had little contact with ministers, who had to determine his wishes, known as 'working towards the Führer', often resulting in contradictions. Hitler disliked paperwork and committees, and did not co-ordinate government. The role of the Cabinet declined – it met 72 times in 1933 but only 4 times in 1936. The last formal meeting was in 1938. This lack of clear leadership often resulted in chaos.

War added to the problems. Hitler was at the Front but would not allow Cabinet meetings or give committees power, as he feared they might challenge him. Decisions were only made by seeing Hitler, and **Bormann** controlled this. Hitler made decisions about foreign policy and dominated government through his charisma, but at times he was unwilling to make decisions.

What was the role of the Nazi Party and the state?

In theory Germany was a one-party, totalitarian state, reinforced by **propaganda**. However, in practice this was not true; there were limits to the power of the Nazi Party because:

- it never destroyed established state institutions
- party divisions remained.

As the bureaucracy of the state was already established and effective, Hitler did not destroy the old institutions such as the ministries, run by civil servants who were often conservative, and the **judiciary**, and never clarified their relationship to the Nazi Party. This led to conflict, overlap and confusion and created **dualism**, where the forces of the Nazi Party, such as the **Hitler Youth**, SS and **Gauleiters**, and the German state co-existed as rival centres of power.

There were attempts to improve party influence after 1938. Hess, as Deputy Führer, insisted civil servants had to be party members and increased party supervision. Bormann created the Department for Internal Party Affairs to discipline the party structure, and the Department for Affairs of State to secure party supremacy over the state.

Linking sources

Below are a question and the four sources referred to in the question. In one colour, draw links between the sources to show ways in which they agree that Hitler was 'master of the Third Reich'. In another colour, draw links between the sources to show ways in which they disagree.

Read Sources A–D. How far do the sources agree that Hitler was 'master of the Third Reich'?

SOURCE A

A leading Nazi explains the power of the Führer.

We must not speak of 'state power' but of 'Führer' power. For it is not the state as an impersonal entity that is the source of political power, but rather political power is given to the Führer as the executor of the nation's common will. 'Führer power' is comprehensive and total.

E. Huber, *The Constitutional Law of the Greater German Empire*, 1939

SOURCE B

A Nazi minister explains how everyone should work towards the Führer.

The Führer can hardly dictate from above everything which he intends to achieve. Everyone with a part in the new Germany has worked best when he has, so to speak, worked towards the Führer. It is the duty of everybody to try to work towards the Führer along the lines he would wish. Those who make mistakes will notice it soon enough. But anyone who really works towards the Führer along the Führer's lines and towards his goal will certainly one day have the finest reward in the confirmation of their work as law.

From a speech by Werner Willikens, State Secretary in the Food Ministry, 1934

SOURCE C

A lawyer explains the problem for ministers in communicating and decision-making within the Nazi regime.

Ministerial skill consisted in making the most of a favourable hour or minute when Hitler made a decision, this often taking the form of a remark thrown out casually, which then went its way as an 'order of the Führer'.

Carl Schmitt, a constitutional lawyer under the Nazi regime

SOURCE D

Hitler's personal assistant describes his daily routine and work habits.

Hitler normally appeared before lunch. He disliked the study of documents. I have sometimes secured decisions from him without his ever asking to see the relevant files. He took the view that many things sorted themselves out on their own if one did not interfere. He let people tell him the things he wanted to hear, everything else he rejected. One still sometimes hears the view that Hitler would have done the right thing if people surrounding him had not kept him wrongly informed.

From the memoirs of Fritz Wiedemann, a personal assistant to Hitler, 1964

Add own knowledge

Annotate Sources A–D with your own knowledge to add evidence that either supports or challenges the views presented in each source about whether Hitler was 'master of the Third Reich'.

The Police State

Revised

The Nazi regime survived largely because it was able to remove its enemies and terrorise its opponents. This was achieved through the creation of a Police State consisting of a variety of groups.

The Courts

- Judges were instructed to issue harsher sentences.
- There were new laws regarding political offences.
- People's Courts were established to try enemies of the state.
- From 1939, judges had to study Nazi beliefs. Judges who did not carry out government wishes were removed.
- Nazis replaced senior officials.
- The SS Group Leader was appointed Minister of Justice.

The SS

Originally established as an elite bodyguard for Hitler in 1925, the SS became a 'state within a state' responsible only to Hitler. It came to dominate the Police State.

In 1929, Himmler became its Head and in 1931 created the **SD** – the secret intelligence wing of the SS. In 1934 he took control of police including the **Gestapo** in Prussia. In 1935 the SS became an elite force that only **Aryans** could join. In 1936, all police and Gestapo powers were placed under Himmler's control. Finally in 1939, all party and state police organisations were amalgamated into the **RSHA**.

The SS was the key organisation in terror. It preserved the Nazi regime and became a key power group. It was made up of the SD, the Gestapo, the **Kripo** and the **Waffen SS**. Their roles included policing, intelligence gathering and, later, military functions. They were responsible for security, **ideology** and race, the economy and a variety of military issues.

The SS were responsible for the creation of the '**New Order**'. Himmler became Commissioner for Consolidating German Nationhood; this gave him responsibility for the resettling of **ethnic Germans** from conquered territories and the elimination of groups such as Jews and gypsies.

The Gestapo

The Gestapo were the secret state police. Their role was to find opponents of the Nazis and arrest them. People arrested could be sent to concentration camps without trial. The Gestapo was a small organisation, with 20,000–40,000 agents, many of whom were little more than office workers who relied on informers and block wardens for information. Wardens were responsible for 50 houses or apartments, and ensured Nazi flags were displayed, and that rallies were attended. There were about 2 million block wardens in Germany. They were unpopular in working-class areas, where there was sympathy for Communists and Socialists.

The impact of war on the Police State

- The role of policing and security expanded.
- The military increased from 3 divisions to 35.
- The 'New Order' was created in occupied lands.
- The process of exterminating and resettling individuals based on ideology and race was developed.

Concentration camps

1933

Concentration camps were prisons where opponents of the regime were questioned and subjected to torture, hard labour and re-education in Nazi ideals. They were established as part of a campaign against Communists and Socialists. Many were closed as they were offensive to nationalists. When Himmler took control there were only 3,000 inmates, suggesting that the campaign to silence opponents had been successful as there were so few.

1936

Camps focused on **asocials**, criminals and homosexuals.

1937

Any individuals who did not fit into the **People's Community** were imprisoned, including beggars, gypsies and the long-term unemployed.

1942

Regular prisoners and foreign workers were transferred to camps as a source of labour. The camps subsequently became extermination camps for Jews.

The numbers held within camps expanded during the war:

September 1939	25,000
December 1942	88,000
January 1945	714,211

High-level answers avoid just summarising or paraphrasing the sources, and instead make inferences from the sources. Below are Source A and a series of statements. Read the source and decide which of the statements:

- make an inference from the source (I)
- paraphrase the source (P)
- summarise the source (S)
- cannot be justified from the source (X).

SOURCE A

A report suggests that the Communists and SPD are having some success.

Communist propaganda is having some success in factories. Many workers only mumble in response to the German salute. The shifting about of workers within the various factories only makes surveillance more difficult and makes it easier for workers to be indoctrinated by Communist activities. It is a similar story with SPD agents. They operate in factories, sports clubs and other organisations. Since the former SPD members carry on propaganda only by word of mouth, it is very difficult to get hold of proof of their illegal activities which would be usable in court. They are too clever and have been trained for too long. The solidarity among them is still strong.

A Gestapo report from Dusseldorf, 1937

Statement	I	P	S	X
The SPD were less successful than the Communists in maintaining support.				
The Communists gained much support among the working class.				
There was a significant amount of opposition to the Nazi regime.				
The Gestapo found it increasingly difficult to monitor the activities of opponents.				
Opposition was well organised.				
The Communists' and Socialists' propaganda was still spread effectively in factories and other clubs.				
The Gestapo was able to successfully prosecute opponents due to the availability of evidence.				
The Nazi regime was weakened by the scale of opposition.				

Resistance

Although the regime collapsed only under the pressure of military defeat and was determined to crush any opposition, many resisted. This resistance took a variety of forms:

- Private grumbling to family and friends or at work.
- Underground resistance and open opposition against the government.
- Attempts to overthrow the regime and remove Hitler.

Why was there so little open opposition?

- 'The Nazi economic miracle': life had improved and many now had jobs and were willing to accept some of the unpopular policies.
- Terror: people were frightened of the Gestapo and concentration camps.
- Opposition groups were divided: Communists and the SPD opposed each other.
- The Nazis abandoned and hid some unpopular policies: criticism after **Kristallnacht** resulted in anti-Jewish measures being performed in secret.

The opposition

Group	Aims and actions	Impact
Communists (most support in industrial cities)	They had cells in large cities. They produced pamphlets attacking the Nazis. Most important was the Red Orchestra, a spy network that sent information to Moscow.	Minimal, as many had been arrested after the Reichstag fire. They were more concerned with self-preservation.
Social Democrats (support in industrial areas among the working class)	Banned as a political party, but retained some underground activity. Their leadership was often arrested. Produced anti-Nazi propaganda and kept the socialist message alive.	Minimal, as their greater concern was self-preservation.
Trade unions (support among factory workers)	They were weakened by arrests after 1933–4 but carried out strikes in 1935–6 and 1945.	Industrial action proved ineffective.
Churches (priests and pastors, individually and as a group)	Bishop Galen of Munster attacked the policy of **euthanasia**. Most adopted a pragmatic response and preserved religious practices.	They did not provide effective opposition, although they were able to stop euthanasia. Many Church leaders were sent to camps.
Youth (those who did not enjoy the activities of the Hitler Youth or resented the loss of freedom)	Groups such as the Swing Youth, Edelweiss Pirates, Roving Dudes and Navajos often just behaved in anti-Nazi ways, such as playing dance and jazz music. They disliked the military emphasis of the Hitler Youth.	Some did attack military targets and assassinate Gestapo officers, but the latter action was limited.
Students	White Rose, a student group in Munich, issued pamphlets condemning the values of the Nazi regime.	Minimal impact – leaders of White Rose were arrested and tortured.
Conservatives (often members of the civil service from the Weimar period)	The Kreisau Circle included officers, aristocrats, academics and churchmen. They drew up plans for post-Nazi Germany.	Some pacifists in the Circle were opposed to a coup. Resistance only developed late on, and it was difficult to organise and plan as they feared arrest.
Army (commanders and high-ranking officers who resented Hitler's background)	There was slow development due to the Army Oath (see page 8) and early military success. However, Army support of Hitler declined after defeat at Stalingrad and opposition developed. Some commanders began to plot and this culminated in the **Bomb Plot** under Stauffenberg.	The Bomb Plot failed and officers were slow to act, allowing Hitler to regain control. About 5000 members of the resistance were killed afterwards.

Support or challenge? ⓐ

Below are an exam-style question that asks how far you agree with a specific statement and a series of general statements. On page 16 is a series of sources that are relevant to the question. Using your own knowledge and the information on the opposite page, decide whether the sources and statements support or challenge the statement in the question and tick the appropriate box.

Using Sources A–E and your own knowledge, how far do you agree with the view that opposition to the Nazi regime was limited in its appeal and effectiveness?

	SUPPORT	CHALLENGE
Source A		
Source B		
Source C		
Source D		
Source E		
Gestapo numbers were limited and this made opposition much easier.		
Opposition lacked organisation and this made it weak.		
Most people simply accepted the regime and were happy that they had work.		
Opposition groups continued to exist throughout the period.		
Pamphlets that opposition groups produced had little impact.		
People were too frightened to listen to messages of opposition.		
There was a large number of different opposition groups.		

Doing reliability well ⓐ

Below are an exam-style question and a series of definitions listing common reasons why sources can be unreliable, and on page 16 are Sources A–E. For each source write a critical account of whether it is a reliable or unreliable support for the view in the question, justifying your answer by referring to the definitions below.

Using the sources and your own knowledge, assess the view that opposition to the Nazi regime was limited in its appeal and effectiveness.

- **Vested interest**: the source is written so that the writer can protect their power or financial interests.
- **Second-hand report**: the writer of the source is not an eyewitness, but is relying on someone else's account.
- **Expertise**: the source is written on a subject in which the author (for example, a historian) is an expert.
- **Political bias**: the source is written by a politician and it reflects their political views.
- **Reputation**: the source is written to protect the writer's reputation.

SOURCE A

A Nazi newspaper comments on the Police State and the enforcement of conformity.

The preventative activity of the secret state police consists primarily in the thorough observation of all enemies of the state in the Reich territory. As the secret state police cannot carry out this observation of the enemies of the state to the extent necessary, there marches by its side to supplement it, the security service of the Reich Führer of the SS. The secret state police takes the necessary police preventative measures on the basis of the results of its observations. The most effective preventative measure is, without doubt, the withdrawal of freedom, which is covered in the form of protective custody.

VolkischerBeobachter, the official Nazi newspaper, January 1936

SOURCE B

A report comments on the growth of Communism in a major German city.

During the first years after the take-over of power, the Communists tried to expand their party. Until 1936 the main KPD propaganda emphasis was on distributing lots of pamphlets. They then switched to propaganda by word of mouth, setting up bases in factories.

A Dusseldorf Gestapo report, published December 1937

SOURCE C

An opponent of the Nazi regime recalls his attempts to resist the Nazi regime in an industrial area of Berlin.

Justice, freedom and culture, and yes socialism, forced us to warn people and arouse their consciences by distributing illegal leaflets and writing slogans on the streets, in public squares and on walls. As late as 1937 we made leaflets in the flat and then scattered them just before dawn from the back of a motorbike on the streets leading to the factories in Berlin. We knew the dangers of what we were doing. There was no heroism; we didn't want to be martyrs. We wanted to survive for the better future we hoped for.

Ludwig Lennert, a member of the SPD

SOURCE D

A German historian writes about life during Nazi rule.

No time for it, when you're on three shift working – with the Labour Front, later on – oh God, yes – people kicked against it a bit and then just carried on, you know! Yes, well obviously, if you were on piecework, you didn't have any time to make speeches, you got up in the morning when you had to, you didn't overstretch your break periods – because after all – the money was tempting. I didn't worry any more about the Nazis, put it that way, apart from my Labour Front contribution I just didn't have anything to do with the Nazis, you know, and anyway I was tied up with my Protestant clubs all week. Nothing really changed there.

Ulrich Herbert, *Good Times, Bad Times: Memories of the Third Reich*, 1986

SOURCE E

A member of the conservative opposition comments on a meeting to discuss resistance to Hitler.

Had conversation with Professor A and M as to what one could do to give public expression to the general abhorrence of these methods, unfortunately without success; without office we have no weapon. Any action on our part would lead to our being silenced or worse.

W has a post at the Vatican which could be important, but which it certainly is not under this regime. He merely lends himself to the Nazis as the usual false front.

The diary of Ulrich von Hassell, November 1938

Exam focus

On pages 18–19 is a sample A-grade answer to the exam-style question below. Read the answer and the examiner comments around it. You could try answering the question below first before looking at the sample answer.

Study Sources A and B. Compare these sources as evidence for the style of Hitler's leadership.

SOURCE A

Hitler's position as Führer was made clear in this speech by the Head of the Nazi Association of Lawyers and the Academy of German Law.

1. At the head of the Reich stands the leader of the NSDAP as leader of the German Reich for life.

2. He is, on the strength of being leader of the NSDAP, leader and Chancellor of the Reich. As such he embodies simultaneously, as Head of State, supreme State power and, as chief of the government, the central functions of the whole Reich administration. He is Head of State and chief of the government in one person. He is Commander in Chief of all the armed forces of the Reich.

3. The Führer and Reich Chancellor is the constituent delegate of the German people, who without regard for formal pre-conditions decides the outward form of the Reich, its structure and general policy.

4. The Führer is supreme judge of the nation. There is no position in the area of constitutional law in the Third Reich independent of the will of the Führer.

Speech by Hans Frank, Head of the Nazi Association of Lawyers, 1938

SOURCE B

Albert Speer, who saw a great deal of Hitler, gives Hitler's own account of his working habits.

In the first few weeks every petty matter was brought to me for decision. Every day I found heaps of files on my desk, and however much I worked there were always as many again. Finally, I put an end to that nonsense. If I had gone on that way, I would never have accomplished anything, simply because that stuff left me no time for thinking. When I refused to see the files they told me important decisions would be held up. But I decided to clear the decks so I could give my mind to important things. That way I governed the course of development instead of being governed by the officials.

Albert Speer, *Inside the Third Reich*, 1970

Study Sources A and B. Compare these sources as evidence for the style of Hitler's leadership.

A good summary of the overall view of the two passages about the key issue in the question. The answer makes it very clear how the passages differ.

Sources A and B give contrasting views of the style of Hitler's leadership; Source A puts forward the view that Hitler ruled as a dictator in a well-organised and structured state, whereas Source B suggests that Hitler himself spent little time on routine government matters and preferred to spend time thinking, suggesting that decision-making was more chaotic.

Note the direct comparison being made between the two sources.

Source A argues that Hitler had limitless powers when he chose to use them, as he was 'Head of State' and 'chief of the government', as well as Commander in Chief and could 'decide the outward form of the Reich, its structure and general policy'. This view of a totalitarian state, however, contrasts with Source B, where Hitler himself states that he was not concerned with routine decisions and the day-to-day running of government, and that his concern was with 'important things' and 'thinking'.

Here the candidate integrates the provenance of the two sources to explain why they offer different views.

Source A is from a speech, the purpose of which was to justify and explain the powers that Hitler had, and would want to give the impression that the state was organised and efficient, making clear the powers that resided in the Führer. This contrasts with Source B, which is written by Speer, who worked closely with Hitler and knew his work habits. As this was written after the collapse of the Nazi regime, Speer did not need to put across an image of a well-run and efficient state, but could record the actual practical running of government. Source A therefore is a theoretical explanation of the powers that Hitler possessed as Führer, whereas Source B is much clearer in showing how the powers were used in practice.

In most instances the two sources chosen will have some subtle point of agreement or disagreement, which stronger candidates will pick up on. Although it is not enough to change the view that the sources disagree, the candidate makes the valid point that the disagreement is not complete.

However, Source B does not completely disagree with Source A, as B implies that Hitler did give his mind to 'important things', suggesting that in some areas he did show concern, such as foreign policy. This supports the view in A that, at least in some areas, he was concerned with 'general policy' and the same view might be drawn from his desire to spend time thinking so that he could determine the 'outward form of the Reich'.

As Source A is from a public speech, Frank will focus on the well-ordered and clearly structured nature of Nazi rule as neither he, nor the Nazis, would want to give the impression that is given in Source B, of a more chaotic government, where Hitler gave little attention to the details of decision-making. The Nazis were very concerned about their image and speeches such as Frank's were part of the regular propaganda that glorified the Führer and upheld the principle of Führerprinzip. However, Source B, written after the collapse of Nazi rule, does not need to justify Nazi government and its methods, but can record the actual practice of Nazi rule, and as Speer also had a house at Berchtesgaden and shared a passion with Hitler for architecture he had the opportunity to see the Führer at work.

Source B is more useful as evidence of Hitler's style of leadership as it is a record of what happened in practice, whereas Source A is partially propaganda designed to give the impression of a totalitarian dictatorship. However, A is useful in showing the wide powers that the Führer possessed if he wanted to use them, whereas B shows what actually happened in practice.

The focus is on provenance, to explain why the sources differ and the points are developed and fully explained.

The candidate reaches a clear judgement. Although the answer concludes that B is the more useful evidence, it also acknowledges the value of A.

28/30

This is a very thorough and well-focused answer, which reaches a clear judgement as to the value of both sources as evidence for the style of Hitler's leadership. The answer has a good balance between the content of the sources and provenance and is able to link both areas back to the key issue in the question set, rather than writing generally about the topic of the sources. The comparison between the two sources is made in a point-by-point approach and the sources are not dealt with sequentially. The candidate considers a range of provenance, looking at origin and purpose. The answer avoids paraphrasing or copying out large chunks of the sources, but uses brief references to support the argument being pursued. Where the candidate brings in own knowledge it is to help explain the source and not simply imparted. This answer was awarded Level I for both AOs.

What makes a good answer?

Make a list of the characteristics that make a good answer. Use the example and examiner comments to help you.

Section 2:
To what extent did the Nazis transform German society?

Changes in society

Revised

Hitler aimed to create a *Volksgemeinschaft* to overcome the divisions of class, religion and politics. This was to be replaced with a collective identity, built on the ideas of race and struggle. Jews, aliens, the mentally sick, the incurably ill and **asocials** were to be excluded.

Education

The Nazis wanted to use education to consolidate the Nazi system and **indoctrinate** the youth with Nazi ideals. In order to achieve their aims teachers had to reinforce Nazi beliefs and values.

How did the educational system change?

- Schools were centralised under the Reich Ministry of Education, Culture and Science.
- '**Unreliables**' were removed from the teaching profession.
- Courses were organised for non-Nazi teachers.
- Headteachers had to be members of the Nazi Party.
- A National Socialist Teachers' League was established.
- The curriculum was changed.

Curriculum changes

More time was given to PE as strength and fitness were essential for producing soldiers. There was increased emphasis on German and History as these emphasised nationalism and heroism. Biology reinforced Nazi **racial genetics** and the population policy. Meanwhile, Religious Studies was dropped as Christianity was seen as unimportant. The Nazis also created schools to produce the Nazi elite:

- The Napolas – state boarding schools run by the **SS**
- Adolf Hitler schools run by the Hitler Youth
- Ordensburgen – a type of school designed to produce the elite for Hitler's future society.

What were the results?

There were many failures in the education programme:

- The Nazis opened few new schools.
- The anti-academic ethos in schools resulted in a fall in standards, which caused resentment, and the professional classes chose to send their children to **grammar schools** rather than **Nazi schools**.
- The numbers joining the teaching profession declined as many disapproved of Nazi **ideology**.

Hitler Youth

Hitler Youth is the term used to describe a range of youth groups in Germany (see table below). The Nazis wanted to use the Hitler Youth to indoctrinate the young, as they were the future of the regime. Membership grew from 1 per cent of children in 1933 to 60 per cent in 1936, and became compulsory in 1939. The Nazis also dissolved all other youth groups, except the **Catholic Youth** movement.

Age	Male	Female
10–14	*Deutsches Jungvolk* (German Young People)	*Jungmadel* (Young Girls League)
14–18	*Hitlerjugend* (Hitler Youth)	*Bund Deutsches Madel* (League of German Girls)

Activities

Boys' activities emphasised the role of a soldier. Girls were taught the role of a wife and mother through domestic activities. Both received political indoctrination – German **patriotism** and the achievements of Hitler were emphasised. With the outbreak of war, youth groups had to help with the harvest, and there was increased military training.

Success?

Many from poorer backgrounds enjoyed the activities. However, the Hitler Youth lost some appeal when it was made compulsory and increased its military emphasis. Those disillusioned with the Hitler Youth set up the Edelweiss Pirates and the Swing Youth (see page 14).

Support or challenge?

Below is a question that asks how far you agree with a specific statement. Below this is a series of general statements that are relevant to the question. Using your own knowledge and the information on the opposite page decide whether these statements support or challenge the statement in the question and tick the appropriate box.

'Nazi education policy was concerned only with teaching military values.' How far do you agree with this statement?

	SUPPORT	CHALLENGE
There was a great deal of emphasis on PE in the Nazi curriculum.		
Girls were taught the importance of being healthy.		
Racial studies formed a key part of the Nazi curriculum.		
In the Hitler Youth, much time was devoted to marching, camping and hiking.		
History lessons were largely about German history from the First World War.		
Nazi ideology was taught in both schools and in the Hitler Youth.		
Maths lessons were often based around the angles of missiles and projectiles or the bombing of Jewish ghettoes.		

Write the question

Sources A and B relate to the young in Germany and their attitudes towards Hitler Youth. Write a part (a) exam-style question (see page 2) using Sources A and B and the information on the page opposite.

SOURCE A

An opposition group comment on the appeal of the Hitler Youth.

Youth is still in favour of the system: the novelty, the drill, the uniform, the camp life, the fact that school and the parental home take a back seat compared to the community of young people – all that is marvellous. Many believe that they will find job opportunities through the persecution of Jews and Marxists. For the first time, peasant youth is associated with the State through the SA and the Hitler Youth. Young workers also join in: one day socialism may come; one is simply trying to achieve it in a new way. The new generation has never had much use for education and reading. Now nothing is demanded of them; on the contrary, knowledge is publicly condemned. The chaps are so fanaticised that they believe in nothing but their Hitler.

Report by the Social Democratic Party in exile, 1934

SOURCE B

A former leader in the Hitler Youth remembers his attitude towards the organisation.

When I became a leader in the Jungvolk the negative aspects became very obvious. I found the compulsion and the requirement of absolute obedience unpleasant. I appreciated that there must be order and discipline in such a large group of boys, but it was exaggerated. It was preferred that people should not have a will of their own and should totally subordinate themselves. When I moved to Bann headquarters and acquired rather more insight I had the first serious doubts. The Hitler Youth was interfering everywhere in people's private lives. If one had private interests apart from the Hitler Youth people looked askance.

A. Klonne, *Youth in the Third Reich*, 1982

Women and the family

The Nazi view of women

The Nazis believed women should look after the family and home. Women were expected to have large families as a growing population was a sign of strength and was needed to supply soldiers. Women had a completely different role to men, and were expected to be devoted to the 'three Ks': kinder, küche and Kirche (children, kitchen and Church).

Under **Weimar**, more women had taken up employment and the birth rate had dropped. The Nazis wanted to reverse both trends.

> ### The ideal Nazi woman
>
> The ideal Nazi woman was blonde, athletic and fit with big hips so as to be able to bear children. She was expected to:
>
> - not smoke
> - avoid the use of make-up
> - wear clothes with full skirts and flat shoes
> - be a good cook and be able to use leftovers to make a one-dish meal at least once a month.

Nazi policies to 1937

In June 1933, women were offered interest-free loans of 600 Reichmarks to marry and give up work. **Labour exchanges** were encouraged to discriminate in favour of men. Women were excluded from politics. The Nazi Women's Organisation was established to put across **anti-feminist ideology**.

In January 1934 the proportion of girls allowed to enter higher education was limited and this was extended in 1937. Grammar school education for girls was abolished and they were banned from learning Latin, a requirement for university.

Nazi policies after 1937

From 1937, Nazi policies had to change because:

- there was a labour shortage
- the **Four Year Plan** required more workers.

As a result of this women were recruited for factory work and they were allowed to rejoin the professions. The number of working women rose from 5.7 million in 1937 to 7.1 million in 1939; the number of female doctors also increased and girls were encouraged to become teachers. Women in work were also allowed marriage loans.

War also meant women were needed for work and by 1942, 52 per cent of the workforce was female. Women also took on military responsibilities as **auxiliaries** by manning searchlights and anti-aircraft batteries.

The family

The Nazis took a series of measures to increase the size of families. This included strict anti-abortion laws and limited contraception advice. They also improved maternity benefits and family allowances, gave marriage loans worth half a year's salary for each child and reduced taxes in proportion to the number of children.

A **propaganda** campaign raised the status of motherhood through rewards such as the 'Mothers Cross' which was given in bronze, silver or gold, depending on the number of children you had. It culminated in the slogan, 'I have donated a child to the *Führer*'.

Lebensborn was introduced in 1935 to improve 'racial standards'. Under this policy, unmarried mothers of 'good racial background' were cared for and **Aryan** girls were impregnated by members of the SS. Around 11,000 children were born under this policy.

Success?

Although the birth rate increased, this may have been due to the end of the Depression. Marriage figures did not increase and divorce rates actually rose. It could be argued that the status of women increased as the role of the mother was seen as important, but women were denied many opportunities.

! Linking sources

Below are a question and Sources A–E. In one colour, draw links between the sources to show ways in which they agree with the statement in the question. In another colour, draw links between the sources to show ways in which they disagree.

Read Sources A–E. How far do the sources agree that 'the main aim of Nazi policy towards women was for them to stay at home and have children'?

SOURCE A

Hitler comments on the role of women in the Nazi state.

If the man's world is said to be the State, his struggle, his readiness to devote his powers to the service of the community, then it may perhaps be said that the woman's is a smaller world. For her world is her husband, her family, her children and her home. The two worlds are not antagonistic. They complement each other, they belong together just as man and woman belong together. We do not consider it correct for the woman to interfere in the world of the man, in his main sphere.

Every child that a woman brings into the world is a battle, a battle waged for the existence of her people.

Hitler's *'Address to Women'* at the Nuremberg Party rally, 8 September 1934

SOURCE B

A leading Nazi outlines the ideal Nazi woman.

We are opposed to women going into the professions which make them 'mannified'. What National Socialists want are women who are genuine comrades and mothers. The ideal woman is one who, above all, is capable of being a mother.

Rudolf Hess, speaking in 1936

SOURCE C

The leader of the SS encourages German women and girls to become mothers.

Beyond the bounds of perhaps otherwise necessary bourgeois law and usage, and outside the sphere of marriage, it will be the sublime task of German women and girls of good blood, acting not frivolously but from a profound moral seriousness, to become mothers to children of soldiers setting off to battle, of whom destiny alone knows if they will return or die for Germany.

An Order from Himmler to the SS, 1940

SOURCE D

A security report comments on the impact of war on married life.

Many women are also concerned that the stability of their marriages and the mutual understanding of their partners is beginning to suffer from the lengthy war. The separation which, with short breaks, has now been going on for years, the transformation in their circumstances through total war and, in addition, the heavy demands which are nowadays made on every individual are changing people. This often produces an increasing distance between the married couple. Having looked forward to being together again during their husband's leave, the occasion is spoilt by frequent rows. That even happens in marriages which were previously models of harmony.

The SS Security Service Report, 18 November 1943

SOURCE E

Two modern historians explain the change in Nazi policies towards women.

By 1936–7, however, as the rearmament boom and the reintroduction of compulsory labour service and conscription in 1935 made themselves felt, a labour shortage began to develop, and it became clear that women provided the main untapped source of labour. In this situation the regime was forced to do an about-turn: having previously discouraged women from going to work, it now had to encourage them to do so.

From two modern historians, J. Noakes and G. Pridham, *Nazism, 1939–45, Volume 2: State, Economy and Society, 1933–39*, published in 1984

The Churches

Christianity and Nazism

Christianity was a major problem for the Nazis. Christianity's teachings directly contradicted the Nazi philosophy of violence, strength and war. Moreover, Jesus was Jewish rather than Aryan, and this went against Nazi *volkisch* beliefs. This was problematic because most Germans were Christians and those with strong religious beliefs were less likely to 'worship' Hitler.

The Protestant Church

Nonetheless, many Christians, especially in the Protestant Church, supported the Nazis because they agreed over family values. Many pastors had spoken in support of the Nazis, encouraging congregations to vote for them, and allowed their churches to be used as Nazi bases.

Co-ordinating the Protestant Church

Hitler wanted to reorganise the Protestant Church as one united Reich Church to make it easier to control, but these plans were resisted. The Nazis appointed Otto Müller, a fanatical Nazi, as Reich Bishop.

Opposition within the Protestant Church

There was some conflict between the Nazis and the Protestant Church. In 1934 two Protestant bishops were arrested for opposing the Reich Church. Pastors then set up the Confessional Church, which was independent of the state. **Pastor Niemöller** led it; he had the support of 7000 out of 17,000 pastors.

The Catholic Church

The Catholic Church was concerned to preserve its independence and signed the **Concordat** in July 1933. This guaranteed religious freedom as the Church could run itself and appoint clergy. Parents could request faith schools for their children. The Nazis also agreed not to interfere with the legal and property rights of the Church. In return the Church agreed to keep out of politics.

The Nazis believed concessions were temporary and later attempted to co-ordinate the Catholic Youth.

The German Faith Movement

As an alternative to Christianity, the Nazis established a **Teutonic paganism**, which:

- upheld a racial belief based on Blood (descent) and Soil (homeland)
- replaced Christian ceremonies with pagan ones
- rejected Christian ethics
- upheld the **cult of** Hitler's **personality**.

Church and state relations

By 1935 the Nazis had failed to co-ordinate the Churches and there was growing opposition within them. It was a problem for the Nazis, as suppression would alienate many Germans, but limited persecution allowed Churches some independence.

The Ministry of Church Affairs adopted polices to undermine the Church. It closed some Church schools, removed crucifixes from others, banned nativity plays and carols from schools and undermined Catholic Youth groups. Campaigns were launched to discredit and harass the clergy – some, such as Niemöller and Bonhoeffer were sent to concentration camps, others were simply prevented from teaching religious classes. Church funds were confiscated making it harder for the Church to function. However, the popularity of priests, such as Bishop Galen who attacked the policy of **euthanasia**, leading to its official suspension, made it difficult for the Nazis to take further action.

At the start of the war the regime wanted to avoid unrest. However, with military success the persecution of the Churches was increased, particularly in the conquered regions.

Success?

Nazi policy had limited success, as only 5 per cent of Germans joined the German Faith Movement. The Churches did compromise to preserve their organisations, and there was some sympathy with Nazism because of traditional values and the dislike of communism.

Spectrum of significance

Below are a question and a list of general points which could be used to answer the question. Use your own knowledge and the information on the opposite page to reach a judgement about the importance of these general points to the question posed. Write numbers on the spectrum below to indicate their relative importance. Having done this, write a brief justification of your placement, explaining why some of these factors are more important than others. The resulting diagram could form the basis of an essay plan.

'The main reason for the failure of Nazi policy towards the Churches was the strength of Christian beliefs within Germany.' How far do you agree with this view?

1. The strength of Christian belief within Germany.
2. The actions of individual churchmen.
3. The lack of support for the German Faith Movement.
4. The Nazis' willingness to compromise with the Churches.
5. Limited persecution did not destroy the Churches.
6. The outbreak of war resulted in a more cautious policy being adopted.

⟵──────────────────────────────────────⟶

Most important
factor

Least important
factor

Explain the difference

The following three sources give different accounts of the impact of the Christian Churches on the Nazi regime. List the ways in which the sources differ. Explain the differences between the sources using the provenance of the sources alone.

SOURCE A

A schoolteacher comments on religious difficulties and a decline in religious practices.

The year 1938 seems to have brought a series of difficulties which have had a negative impact on the general attitude of the parishes. The work of our ministers has become much more difficult than before. The danger which threatens our parishes is that of being ground down and paralysed by the National Socialists. Most teachers have given up on religious instruction since it has been removed from the core curriculum. State Youth organisations take less and less account of spiritual matters. The regime is putting obstacles in the way of religious instruction. The population, and above all young people, are losing the habit of going to church.

An account from a local Nazi schoolteacher when, in 1938, fifty parents demanded she be sacked

SOURCE B

A local report comments on church attendance.

Although the young are still staying away, more and more people are going to church. There are unanimous reports that both Catholic and Protestant Churches are engaging in exceptionally heavy activity. In comparison to the party, the Churches today still have much manpower at their disposal.

Report in 1938 by leading Ministers of the Protestant Church on relations between the Church and Nazi regime in Bavaria

SOURCE C

A Nazi report outlines the influence of the Church.

In their weekly reports party organisations have repeatedly emphasised that both Churches, but especially the Catholics, are in today's fateful struggle one of the main pillars of negative influence upon public morale. This is despite our attempts to restrict religious teaching.

An official Nazi report from Gauleiters in June 1943 on the attitudes and behaviour of Christian Churches during wartime

Propaganda and control

The Nazis did not just rely on terror and repression to maintain control. Propaganda was used to win over the public and help create a *Volksgemeinschaft* through:

- glorifying the war and the Aryan race
- spreading Nazism and Nazi values.

It was also used in wartime in order to mobilise people, sustain morale and provide practical advice on air-raids, recycling, food and 'careless talk'.

Responsibility for propaganda was given to Goebbels, who was made Minister of Public Enlightenment and Propaganda. Departments were established to run the press, film, radio and theatre. They censored all non-Nazi culture and media and promoted Nazi ideology.

Historians have usually assumed that Nazi propaganda was very successful, but recent work based on local studies has shown that the degree of success varied according to the purpose. It did help to create the Hitler myth and strengthen Germany, but was less successful in creating a Nazi culture and winning over the working classes.

Examples of propaganda

Radio

Goebbels brought broadcasting under Nazi control and created the Reich Radio Company. As only 25 per cent of Germans owned radios, the government produced cheap sets – the People's Receiver. By 1939, 70 per cent of the population had radios.

There was no escaping the Nazi message as loudspeakers were installed in factories, cafes and offices. 'Radio wardens' co-ordinated listening. However, Goebbels was aware that too much political propaganda bored people; therefore two-thirds of airtime was popular songs and music.

Mass communication was directly under the regime's control.

Press

Germany had a tradition of independent newspapers. Goebbels closed down Socialist and Communist ones and placed others under the control of the Reich Press Chamber. The Editor's Law of 1933 ensured papers reported Nazi views and editors were punished if they went against this. A daily press conference at the Propaganda Ministry gave editors guidance on what to write. News agencies were also placed under state control to ensure they put forward a pro-Nazi view.

Drama and music

The Nazis wanted drama and music to uphold Nazi values and therefore they exercised strict control over them. Theatres and plays had to have a license and were subject to police supervision. They banned experimental plays and music. In music even some classics were censored, jazz was forbidden as it was degenerate and music by Jews was forbidden, while Jewish conductors and musicians were dismissed.

Literature and art

Writers had to be positive about Nazism. There were approved themes, such as the early days of Nazism, war and expansion. The Reich Chamber of Literature listed banned books, and libraries and second-hand bookshops were raided.

Modernist art was banned and modern paintings were removed from galleries. Acceptable art portrayed the German countryside and heroic German warriors.

Film

The Reich Film Chamber was established and everyone in the film industry had to join. There were few political films, but the Weekly Review contained political information and had to be included in all film programmes.

Ritual

Rituals were used to unite society, strengthen the regime, win popularity and glorify the Nazi past. The regime created new social rituals such Heil Hitler. Other examples included:

- the **Horst Wessel** anthem
- uniforms
- public festivals to commemorate the Seizure of Power, the Party Foundation, Hitler's birthday and the Munich *Putsch*.

Below are a series of definitions listing common reasons why sources can be unreliable, and a series of sources. Under each source, explain why the source is either reliable or unreliable for the purpose stated, justifying your answer by referring to the following definitions.

- **Vested interest**: the source is written so that the writer can protect their power or financial interest.
- **Second-hand report**: the writer of the source is not an eyewitness, but is relying on someone else's account.
- **Expertise**: the source is written on a subject in which the author (for example, a historian) is an expert.
- **Political bias**: the source is written by a politician and it reflects their political views.
- **Reputation**: the source is written to protect the writer's reputation.

SOURCE A

An American journalist in Germany reports on the reaction of ordinary Germans to a speech by Hitler.

I remember being in a big Berlin café when it was announced that Hitler was to speak on the radio. The loudspeaker was turned on. Next to me was a group of German businessmen. They went on talking in low voices. At another table was a woman writing a letter. She went on writing. The only man who stood up was a small man with his tie creeping over his collar at the back of his neck. No one else in the crowded café listened to Adolf Hitler.

Philip Gibbs, writing in 1934

> The source is reliable/unreliable as a description of the effectiveness of Nazi propaganda because
>
> _____
>
> _____
>
> _____

SOURCE B

A description of the roll-call of Political Wardens (Heads of local party groups) at the 1936 Nuremberg Rally.

We have witnessed many great march-pasts and ceremonies. But none of them was more thrilling, and at the same time more inspiring, than yesterday's roll call of 140,000 political wardens, who were addressed by the Führer at night, on the Zeppelin Meadow which floodlights had made as bright as day. It is hardly possible to let words describe the mood and strength of this hour.

Reported in *Niederelbisches Tageblatt* (a local newspaper), 1936

> The source is reliable/unreliable as a description of the effectiveness of Nazi propaganda because
>
> _____
>
> _____
>
> _____

'Racial purity'

At the centre of Nazi ideology was the idea of a 'racially pure state'; therefore some groups of people were excluded from *Volksgemeinschaft*. Those excluded were considered to be 'biologically inferior' or sub-human (***Untermenschen***) and of 'lesser racial value'. They were discriminated against and persecuted.

This ideology was based on **Social Darwinism** and the survival of the fittest. The Nazis believed:

■ Aryans (***Herrenvolk***) were the superior race. They were superior because of their intelligence, hard work and willingness to make sacrifices for the nation.

■ Germany lost the First World War because of the weak, and to become strong the weak had to be removed and not produce children.

■ Mixing with the *Untermenschen* had contaminated Aryans. To achieve racial purity, selective breeding and removal of undesirables was required.

■ The ideal German was socially useful and contributed to the state. The **workshy**, unhealthy, disabled, mentally handicapped, tramps, beggars and asocials were seen as worthless, unproductive and dangerous, as they did not fit the Nazi ideal.

Policies

The Nazis introduced a range of policies against those who did not fit into the Nazi ideal.

1. A propaganda campaign against undesirables, aiming to create resentment.

2. A sterilisation law in 1933: 'The Law for the Prevention of Hereditary Diseased Offspring'. This allowed the sterilisation of the 'simple minded' and 'chronic alcoholics', but also of sufferers of schizophrenia, Huntington's chorea, hereditary blindness and deafness. From 1934 onwards, about 350,000 men were sterilised.

3. The Law against Dangerous Habitual Criminals, November 1933, introduced compulsory castration for certain sexual offenders.

4. A department within the **Gestapo** was established to deal with homosexuals. A law was introduced in 1935 and was co-ordinated by Reich Central Office for the Combating of Homosexuality and Abortion. This resulted in the arrest of 50,000 homosexuals.

5. By 1936 the workshy, tramps, beggars, prostitutes, homosexuals and juvenile delinquents were sent to concentration camps.

6. Euthanasia campaign, 1939. The Nazis started to exterminate the mentally ill and removed 6000 handicapped babies, children and teenagers. Targeted disabilities included Down's syndrome and cerebral palsy. No law allowed it, but it was carried out under 'Operation T4'. Gas chambers were built at six mental asylums. By 1941, when protests forced the programme to be stopped, 72,000 people had been killed. It was re-started secretly and was extended to foreign workers with incurable physical illness, 'racially inferior' babies and terminally sick prisoners.

7. Asocials who were orderly were often put into compulsory labour, but the disorderly were imprisoned, sterilised or subjected to medical experiments.

Racial policy developed with the war and expanded east where, according to the Nazis, large numbers of *Untermenschen* lived.

Gypsies

Gypsies were persecuted as non-Aryan, workshy and homeless. The Nazis feared them mixing with Aryans.

● In 1935 gypsies were banned from marrying Germans. The SS Research Unit concluded that they were of mixed race and were likely to have criminal and asocial tendencies, therefore they should be sterilised.

● In 1938 the Decree for the 'Struggle against the Gypsy Plague' was issued. All gypsies were registered, ensuring racial separation from Germans.

● In 1939, 30,000 gypsies were deported to special sites in Poland. During the war, most were sent to concentration camps.

Mind map

Make a copy of the mind map below and use the information on the opposite page to add detail. Add information about Nazi policies towards these groups and their reasons for persecuting them.

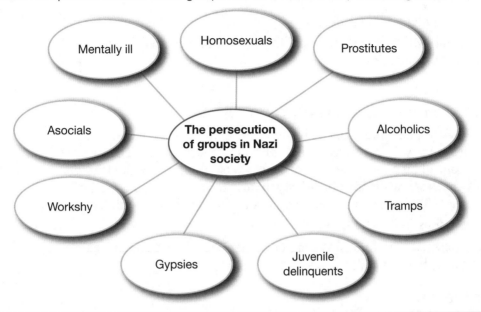

Spot the inference

High-level answers avoid just summarising or paraphrasing the sources, and instead make inferences from the sources. Below are a source and a series of statements. Read the source and decide which of the statements:

- make an inference from the source (I)
- paraphrase the source (P)
- summarise the source (S)
- cannot be justified from the source (X).

SOURCE A

A Nazi ideologist outlines his policy to achieve pure Germans.

'The new aristocracy will arise in this way. We will gather in the best blood only,' said Darre pointing to his iron filing-cabinets. 'Just as we have again produced the old Hanover type of horses from sires and dams who had little of the old purity left, so we shall again, in the course of generations breed the type of the Nordic German by means of recessive crossing. Perhaps we shall not be able to purify the whole of the German nation again. But the new German aristocracy will be a pure breed in the literal sense of the term.'

W. Darre, quoted in H. Rauschning, *Hitler Speaks*, 1939

Statement	I	P	S	X
Nazi racial policy was a success.				
The Nazis wanted to introduce a policy of selective breeding similar to that used in farming.				
Nazi racial policy aimed to purify the German nation.				
Nazism had no place for weakness and wanted to remove it from German society.				
Only the pure-blooded would be allowed to breed so as to remove weaker elements.				
The Nazis wanted only pure-bred Germans as part of the nation.				

Anti-Semitism

Nazi policy towards the Jews went through three phases:

- origins: the development of Nazi ideology
- gradualism: during 1933–9 there was legal discrimination, increased terror, violence and forced emigration
- **genocide**.

Anti-Semitism: origins and gradualism

Anti-Semitism was not new in European history, and in the nineteenth and early twentieth centuries Jews were portrayed as inferior to the German race. This anti-Semitism was enhanced by people looking for scapegoats for Germany's defeat in the First World War (the **'Stab in the back' myth**) and for the economic crisis of the 1920s and early 1930s. The Nazis used this situation to develop an anti-Semitic ideology which led to persecution of the Jewish people.

During the 1930s persecution of the Jews happened gradually, first through legal means and then through terror and violence.

Legal discrimination

Laws gradually removed the rights of Jews. The campaign was supported by propaganda, such as posters, newspapers (*der Sturmer*) and films (*The Eternal Jew*).

Some anti-Jewish measures

- 1 April 1933: the **Boycott** of Jewish Shops. This was not widely accepted.
- 7 April 1933: Law of Restoration of the Professional Civil Service excluded Jews from the civil service.
- 1935: The Nuremberg Race Laws included:
  - the Reich Citizenship Act, which led to Jews losing their citizenship
  - the Law for the Protection of German Blood and German Honour, which forbade marriage between Germans and Jews.
- 1938: Jewish doctors were not allowed to practise.
- 1938: Polish Jews were expelled from Germany.
- 1938: Jews were excluded from schools and universities.
- 1938: The compulsory closure and sale of Jewish businesses.

Violence

From 1934–8 violence against Jews was localised and sporadic. However, in March 1938 there were attacks on 200,000 Jews in Vienna, Austria and on 9–10 November 1938 there was a co-ordinated campaign of violence across Germany known as *Kristallnacht* when Jewish homes, businesses and synagogues were attacked.

Emigration

In 1938 the Central Office for Jewish Emigration in Vienna was established, under Eichmann, to force Jews to emigrate, followed by the establishment of the Reich Central Office for Jewish Emigration in 1939. This led to about half the Jews leaving before the war.

Add own knowledge

Below are an exam-style question and Sources A–E. In one colour, draw links between the sources to show ways in which they agree about support for Nazi policy towards the Jews. In another colour, draw links between the sources to show ways in which they disagree. Around the edge of the sources, write relevant own knowledge. Again, draw links to show the ways in which this agrees and disagrees with the sources.

How far do you agree with the view that Nazi policy towards the Jews was supported by the German people? Explain your answer, using Sources A–E and your own knowledge.

SOURCE A

An opponent explains people's reaction to the early persecution of the Jews.

The Jewish laws are not taken very seriously because the population has other problems on its mind and is mostly of the opinion that the whole fuss about the Jews is only being made to divert people's attention from other things and to provide the SA with something to do. But one must not imagine that the anti-Jewish agitation does not have the desired effect on many people. There are enough people who are influenced by the defamation of the Jews and regard them as the originators of many bad things. But the vast majority ignore this defamation and prefer to buy in Jewish department stores and adopt a really unfriendly attitude to the SA men on duty there.

A report by a Social Democrat supporter in Saxony, 1935

SOURCE B

A Socialist Party agent reports on anti-Jewish activity in Saxony, a notably anti-Semitic area.

Anti-Semitism has undoubtedly taken root in wide circles of the population. If people nevertheless buy from Jews, then it is not in order to help the Jews but to annoy the Nazis. The general anti-Semitic feeling affects even thoughtful people, our comrades as well. All are decided opponents of violence. People are, however, in favour of breaking once and for all the supremacy of the Jews and restricting them to certain activities. Fundamentally people agree to a large extent with Hitler. The Jews have become too influential.

A Socialist Party report produced in 1936

SOURCE C

Goebbels gives his reaction to Kristallnacht.

The justifiable and understandable indignation of the German people at the cowardly murder of a German diplomat in Paris was widely displayed last night. In numerous towns and villages of the Reich, reprisals were carried out against Jewish buildings and places of business. The whole population is now firmly asked to abstain from all further action of whatever nature against the Jews. The final reply to the Jewish outrage in Paris will be given to the Jews by legal means.

Joseph Goebbels, press statement about the events of *Kristallnacht*, 10 November 1938

SOURCE D

An opposition group comment about the different attitudes towards Jews.

The broad mass of the people has not condoned the destruction, but we should nevertheless not overlook the fact that there are people among the working class who do not defend the Jews. There are certain circles where you are not very popular if you speak disparagingly about the recent incidents (Kristallnacht) … Berlin: the population's attitude was not fully unanimous. If there has been any speaking out in the Reich against the Jewish pogroms, the excesses of arson and looting, it has been in Hamburg and the neighbouring Elbe district. People from Hamburg are not generally anti-Semitic, and the Hamburg Jews have been assimilated far more than Jews in other parts of the Reich.

From a report by the Social Democratic Party in exile, December 1938

SOURCE E

A prominent Nazi official explains his feelings about anti-Semitism.

The people had a tendency to anti-Semitism at that time. The Jews had a particularly strong influence on cultural life, and their influence seemed to me particularly dangerous in this sphere because tendencies which I felt to be definitely un-German and inartistic, appeared as a result of Jewish influence, especially in the spheres of painting and music. The Reich Chamber of Culture Law was created, radically excluding the Jews from German cultural life, but with the possibility of making exceptions. I applied these exceptions whenever I was in a position to do so. The law, as I have stated, was decreed by the Reich Cabinet, which bears the responsibility for it.

Walter Funk, former Nazi Minister for Economic Affairs, interviewed in *Trial of German Major War Criminals*, 1946

Anti-Semitism: genocide

War

The German occupation of Poland in 1939 brought 3 million Jews under Nazi control. War made resettlement difficult and therefore **ghettoes** were created.

1941

In June 1941, following the invasion of Russia, SS *Einsatzgruppen* followed the invading army and rounded up Jews. They carried out mass shootings, murdering 700,000 Jews in 1941–2. From September 1941 Jews had to wear the yellow Star of David so they were easily identified. The practical problem of fighting the war and dealing with the number of Jews resulted in Nazi leadership finding a '**Final Solution**'.

The Final Solution

The Final Solution was agreed at **Wannsee** in January 1942. The policy had changed from resettlement to extermination. The Final Solution outlined plans to use gas for extermination and resulted in the development of Extermination Centres at Auschwitz, Sobibor and Treblinka. Jews were moved from the ghettoes to death camps.

In 1943 the Warsaw ghetto was destroyed and the Jews were transported to death camps. In 1944 Jews from all over German-conquered lands were transported to death camps.

Was the Final Solution planned?

There is much historical debate as to whether the Final Solution was planned from the start.

Those who uphold this argument believe that Hitler was committed to the extermination of the Jews from early in his career and followed a consistent policy of gradually increasing persecution, resulting in extermination because that is what he wanted. Some have even suggested that the Holocaust was intended because many Germans took part in it.

However, an examination of events suggests that the implementation was haphazard, as there were no written orders for the killing of the Jews. This suggests that the policy was only decided at the end of 1941 and agreed at Wanssee in January 1942.

Doing reliability well

Below are a series of definitions listing common reasons why sources can be unreliable and a series of sources. Reread Sources C, D and E on page 31 and explain why each source is either reliable or unreliable for the purpose stated, justifying your answer by referring to the following definitions.

- **Vested interest**: the source is written so that the writer can protect their power or financial interest.
- **Second-hand report**: the writer of the source is not an eyewitness, but is relying on someone else's account.
- **Expertise**: the source is written on a subject in which the author (for example, a historian) is an expert.
- **Political bias**: the source is written by a politician and it reflects their political views.
- **Reputation**: the source is written to protect the writer's reputation.

Source C

The source is reliable/unreliable as a description of support for Nazi policy towards the Jews because

---

Source D

The source is reliable/unreliable as a description of support for Nazi policy towards the Jews because

---

Source E

The source is reliable/unreliable as a description of support for Nazi policy towards the Jews because

Exam focus

On pages 35–7 is a sample A-grade answer to the exam-style question below. Read the answer and the examiner comments around it. You could try answering the question below first before looking at the sample answer.

> Study all the sources. Use your own knowledge to assess how far the sources support the view that Hitler had a long-standing determination to exterminate the Jewish population of Europe.

SOURCE A

Early in his political career Hitler discusses his hatred for the Jews.

If, at the beginning of the war and during the war, twelve or fifteen thousand of these Hebrew corrupters of the people had been held under poison gas, as happened to hundreds of thousands of our best German brothers in the field, the sacrifice of millions at the Front would not have been in vain.

Adolf Hitler, an extract from *Mein Kampf*, written in 1924 while in prison

SOURCE B

*In a speech to the **Reichstag** Hitler warns that if war breaks out it will be the responsibility of the Jews.*

Today I will once more be a prophet: if the international Jewish financiers in and outside Europe should succeed in plunging the nation once more into a world war, then the result will not be the Bolshevising of the earth, and thus the victory of Jewry, but the annihilation of the Jewish race in Europe!

Hitler's speech to the Reichstag, 30 January 1939

SOURCE C

Instructions to the German army on what to do with the large number of Jews they captured as they advanced further east.

To supplement the task that was assigned to you on 24 January 1939, which dealt with the Jewish problem by emigration and evacuation in the most suitable way, I hereby charge you with making all necessary preparations with regard to organisational, technical and material matters for bringing about a complete solution of the Jewish question within the German sphere of influence in Europe.

Directive on the Jewish problem, 31 July 1941

SOURCE D

In November 1941 Heydrich had been given the responsibility to draw up plans for the complete solution of the Jewish question in Europe.

In pursuance of the Final Solution, the Jews will be conscripted for labour to the East under appropriate supervision. Large labour gangs will be formed from those fit for work, with the sexes separated, which will be sent to those areas for road construction and undoubtedly a large number of them will drop out through natural wastage. The remainder who survive – and they will certainly be those who have the greatest powers of endurance – will have to be dealt with accordingly. For if released, they would, as a natural selection of the fittest, form a germ cell from which the Jewish race could regenerate itself (that is the lesson of history).

In the process of carrying out the Final Solution, Europe will be combed through and through from west to east. The evacuated Jews will be initially brought in stages to so-called transit ghettoes in order to be transported from there further east.

An extract of the minutes of the Wannsee Conference, prepared by Eichmann, 1941

Rudolf Hess explains how and when the implementation of the Final Solution began.

In the summer of 1941, I was suddenly summoned to see Himmler, the Reichsführer SS. He received me on his own and said: 'The Führer has ordered that the Jewish question be solved once and for all. The SS are to implement this order. The existing extermination centres in the East are in no position to carry out the anticipated large actions. I have therefore earmarked Auschwitz for this purpose.'

From the testimony of Rudolf Hess at the Nuremberg War Crimes Trials, 1946

Study all the sources. Use your own knowledge to assess how far the sources support the view that Hitler had a long-standing determination to exterminate the Jewish population of Europe.

Sources B, D and E suggest that Hitler wanted the removal or 'annihilation' of the Jews in Europe. Source C also hints at the development of a plan for the 'complete solution' of the Jewish question, but this follows from 'emigration' and 'evacuation', suggesting that the extermination was not a long-term plan. Source A makes little mention of the extermination of the Jewish population, but does show that Hitler had a long-standing hatred of the Jews, blaming them for Germany's defeat in the First World War and suggesting that if some had been gassed then Germany's problems may have been avoided.

Sources D and E provide the clearest indication that Hitler had a plan for the extermination of the Jewish population in Europe. Source D argues that there needed to be a plan to deal with those that survived the labour gangs, and that they would 'have to be dealt with accordingly' to prevent the Jewish race from regenerating. Source E explains how this would happen through 'existing extermination centres in the East', but also through the development of Auschwitz. Although both sources argue that the Jews were to be exterminated they do not provide evidence of a long-term plan; both sources are written about events in 1941 and 1942 and make no mention of an earlier plan, although E suggests that extermination centres already existed. However, Source E is from the testimony of Hess at the Nuremberg War Crimes Trials and he would have wanted to play down any suggestion that a long-term plan was implemented as he wanted to show that he was not involved to ensure his punishment was as light as possible. He claims that he was 'suddenly summoned', suggesting that the plan had only just been drawn up. This view is given further credence in Source D, the minutes of the Wannsee Conference, which sets out the plan for the Final Solution. As Heydrich had been given responsibility for the Final Solution only in November 1941 it again suggests that this was not a long-term plan. The timing of the plan is best explained by the German invasion of Russia in the summer of 1941 as this brought German forces into contact with large numbers of Jews, who in

Groups the sources in a sensible fashion. It is essential that sources are grouped and dealt with as groups, rather than sequentially, if the top levels are to be achieved.

A good example of the integration of sources, own knowledge and provenance. However, the answer does start from the sources and candidates do need to remember that this is a source paper and answers should be source driven.

In assessing the provenance of Sources D and E, the candidate refers to both the origin and purpose of the sources and uses the reliability of four to challenge the view that Hess' account is unreliable. Cross-referencing helps to prevent an answer from handling each source discretely.

The use of own knowledge is linked clearly to the argument and the knowledge deployed is precise with reference to the invasion of Russia in 1941.

a time of war could not be moved or resettled without hindering the war effort, hence the need for the Final Solution. As minutes of the meeting they are likely to provide a reliable record of what was decided as Eichmann would need an accurate record and would have no reason in early 1942 to distort the truth, unlike Hess. However, the fact that Eichmann's minutes agree with Hess suggests that the Final Solution was not a long-term plan.

Once again the paragraph starts from the source. Although Source C is considered in a separate paragraph, it is linked back to the previous one.

Source C appears to provide further support for this view as it argues that in January 1939 the Jewish problem was to be solved by 'emigration' and 'evacuation', but that in 1941 instructions were issued to change policy to bring about a 'complete solution'. As this is a directive on the Jewish problem it will explain policy accurately and supports the view that the change was due more to the invasion of Russia than any long-term plan. The comments about 'emigration' and 'evacuation' are also given further credence by the actual policies pursued by the Nazis during these years. In the first years of the war Jews had been placed in ghettoes such as Warsaw and had been resettled in the East. There was even consideration of resettling all Jews in Madagascar, which does not suggest that at this point there were plans for the annihilation of the Jewish population.

Own knowledge is used well to link specific issues raised in Source C, 'emigration' and 'evacuation', to actual policies, such as the establishment of ghettoes. Once again, a precise example is provided.

However, Sources C, D and E all agree that once the extermination had been decided, plans with clear directives and instructions were then drawn up. Source C calls for the 'necessary preparations with regard to organisational, technical and material matters', while D states that 'Europe will be combed through and through' and that 'evacuated Jews will be initially brought in stages to so-called transit ghettoes' and E mentions the need to develop a further centre, Auschwitz.

This paragraph reaches an interim judgement and makes it clear to an examiner the direction in which the argument is going.

Provides the other side of the argument, ensuring that both sides have been considered in a balanced approach.

However, the view that the Final Solution was a later response to the increased numbers of Jews the German army was faced with is challenged by Source B, where Hitler, as early as January 1939, called for the annihilation of the Jewish race. It could be argued that this follows from his comments in Source A when, in Mein Kampf, he mentions the benefits that Germany would have received from the gassing of 'twelve or fifteen thousand of these Hebrew corrupters'. Although both these sources were written by Hitler neither offers a reliable view of his policies. Source A was written when he was in jail and the Nazi Party had no chance of coming to power and represents his thoughts about Jews and how he blamed them for all of Germany's problems, rather than offering a coherent policy that he would implement. As the leader of a marginal, extremist party, Hitler did not need to have a coherent plan, but instead dramatic rants that might win support would be of more use. This is similar to Source B where Hitler is trying to deflect blame for the likely outbreak of war onto the Jews, rather than the result of his own expansionist policies,

The candidate makes good use of brief quotations from the sources to support their argument, but does not copy out large sections, showing that they are able to select relevant material to support their line of argument.

hence his comment that 'if the international Jewish financiers in and outside Europe should succeed in plunging the nation once more into a world war', they would be annihilated. As with Source A, Hitler is trying to convince people that the Jews were to blame and win support for his anti-Semitic policies and justify a future war that many in Germany did not want after the defeat and suffering of the First World War, therefore exaggerating their impact. The Reichstag, since 1934, had become little more than a place from which Hitler gave pronouncements, rather than the centre of discussion, and this speech is typical of the development as he used it largely for propaganda purposes. Nazi policy in the earlier period would also suggest that there was no long-term plan for the extermination, as despite the increased violence of Kristallnacht, Jews had been encouraged to leave Germany and their lives had been made difficult by a series of laws restricting employment and removing their citizenship, but there was no indication that this would change.

The evidence for a long-term plan is not supported by the sources. The sources suggest that the plan was devised during the war and in response to a particular problem: the number of Jews encountered as the German army moved further east. Although Sources A and B show that Hitler disliked the Jews, they were used by him as a scapegoat to win support and his writings and speeches against them are designed to win support for the party and offer the German people someone to blame for their problems, rather than evidence of a coherent plan to exterminate them.

> The evaluation of the reliability is well developed and there is detailed consideration of the purpose of both sources.

> The candidate reaches a clear judgement, which follows from the rest of the answer and has been supported throughout. The candidate does not suddenly offer a view that contradicts the earlier comments.

64/70

This is well-focused on the question and always links both the source material and own knowledge back to the actual question set. The answer addresses the issue of 'long-standing', rather than whether there was a plan to exterminate the Jews. All the sources are used, but not sequentially or discretely as the answer groups the sources in a coherent manner. There is much cross-referencing between sources to support the argument being pursued. The own knowledge that is deployed is integrated with the sources and is used to help assess the reliability of the views offered in the sources, rather than simply added on at the end. The answer assesses the reliability of each source, but again as groups, and these points are fully developed, rather than relying on sweeping generalisations. In assessing the reliability of the sources the candidate considers a range of provenance, looking at origin and purpose. The answer avoids paraphrasing or copying out large chunks of the sources, but uses brief references to support the argument being pursued. Although the candidate considers both sides of the argument, a consistent argument is followed and the answer reaches a judgement based on a full evaluation of the sources. The answer was awarded Level 1 for both AO1 and AO2.

> **Understanding the demands of the question**
>
> In different colours, underline examples where the answer uses own knowledge, evaluates, quotes from the sources and cross-references the sources.

Section 3:
To what extent and in what ways did Communism transform the GDR?

The Potsdam Conference

The Allies agreed to divide Germany into four zones at the Yalta conference in February 1945. They met again at Potsdam in July 1945. This conference was attended by Soviet leader Stalin, US **President** Truman and British Prime Ministers Churchill and Atlee. There were disagreements between Russia and the other allies over boundaries and **reparations**, which helped form a divided Germany in the long term.

What was agreed?

- Germany was to be administered under joint Allied control and was divided into four zones of occupation, as was Berlin.
- Germany was to be demilitarised, **de-Nazified** and democratised.
- Elections were to be held, starting at local government level, to give Germany the 'chance to rebuild its life on a democratic and peaceful basis'.
- Poland gained much former German land; the **Oder-Neisse line** formed the border between Poland and the Soviet zone.
- Germans in Poland, Hungary and Czechoslovakia were repatriated to Germany.
- The economy was to be run as one unit and each occupying force was to take reparations from their zone of occupation.
- As the Soviet zone had fewer resources, they were allowed an additional 25 per cent of reparations from the British and American zones.

The Soviet zone

Demilitarisation

German forces disbanded after their surrender in May 1945. As there was no German government, there could be no independent German military force. This remained until 1955.

De-Nazification

The Nazi Party was disbanded and major war criminals were tried at Nuremberg. The Soviet zone interned large numbers of former Nazis, many of whom died in the former concentration camps where they were held. Later, 'nominal' Nazis who committed themselves to communism returned to political life. The Soviets argued that Nazism resulted from **capitalism**, therefore it had to be destroyed:

- Large landed estates were confiscated and redistributed among landless agricultural labourers.
- Former Nazis' property was taken; some was kept by the state.
- A similar process was adopted later for banks and factories.
- Some equipment was dismantled and taken back to Russia as reparations. Russia also removed experts to reconstruct the technical equipment in Russia.

Democratisation

German Communists, led by Walter Ulbricht, arrived in Berlin at the end of April 1945. They planned to gain control in Berlin, but give the appearance of democracy.

The Soviet Military Administration (SMAD) issued Order No 2 on 10 June 1945, which licensed the formation of political parties. All parties were brought together in an anti-fascist bloc, or National Front, against Nazism in July 1945.

The KPD or Communist Party was established, followed by the Social Democratic Party (SPD). These merged in 1946 to form the Socialist Unity Party (SED). The SPD distrusted Communist policy and its links with the army, but agreed to unite as they saw it was the only way for them to influence policy.

Liberal parties also merged to form the Liberal Democratic Party of Germany (LDPD). The Catholic Centre Party and Protestant parties formed the Christian Democratic Union (CDU).

At first, it appeared as if the Communist Party would adopt a democratic approach, but by 1948 it had formally abandoned democracy.

Spot the inference

High-level answers avoid summarising or paraphrasing the sources, and instead make inferences from the sources. Below are a source and a series of statements. Read the source and decide which of the statements:

- make an inference from the source (I)
- paraphrase the source (P)
- summarise the source (S)
- cannot be justified from the source (X).

SOURCE A

A communiqué explains the seizure of property that formerly belonged to Nazis and their future punishment.

By the Order of the Supreme Chief of the Soviet Military Administration and Commander-in-Chief of the Soviet Occupation Army in Germany of 21 May 1946, all confiscated and sequestered trade and industrial enterprises which belonged to the Hitler state and its organs, to the Nazi Party and its affiliated bodies, or to activist Nazis and war criminals have, under the above Order, been expropriated and put at the disposal of the Administration of Land Saxony. The Land Administration has agreed to the proposal of the anti-fascist democratic parties and trade unions to hold a referendum to decide on the disposal of this property. The purpose of the referendum is the punishment of those guilty of the Nazi regime and of the imperialist predatory war brought about by Nazism and the deprivation of such persons of the economic power once again to plunge the German people into a criminal war with all its fateful consequences for them and for the peoples of Europe.

From Beate Ruhm von Oppen (ed.), *Documents on Germany under Occupation 1945–1954*, published 1955

Statement	I	P	S	X
There was a determination to punish former Nazis by taking away their economic power.				
The Communists wanted to appear democratic.				
The industrial activities of former Nazis have been put at the disposal of the new administration.				
It was the Nazis who plunged Europe into war, and they should be punished.				
Democratic practices were already in place in Saxony.				
The Soviet forces appeared to be reasonable by allowing a referendum.				
The Soviets wanted to win popular support through their policies.				
There was much former Nazi property to be disposed of.				

The consolidation of Communism under the SED

The SED was the leading Communist party in the East and led by Walter Ulbricht. It claimed to be a liberator from fascism and argued that ordinary workers and peasants were innocent of Nazism and war guilt. The property of absentee factory owners, Nazis, war criminals and **Junkers** was confiscated. This helped the SED to win popular support.

The founding statement of the SED claimed it was wrong to impose the Soviet system and called for 'the establishment of an anti-fascist, democratic regime, a parliamentary-democratic republic'.

Initially the Communist Party encouraged the development of parties with which they could work, but the SED increasingly gained control of other parties in the Soviet zone and set up two new parties, the National Democratic Party, aimed at former Nazis, and the Democratic Peasants Party of Germany, aimed at peasants.

All parties agreed that state control and economic intervention was needed, and this gave Communist plans and the Communist Party further support.

How did the Communists dominate the Eastern zone?

Initially the Communist party did not have mass support and could not control all areas of life. In some areas of East Germany non-Communists were appointed as mayors. However, the Communists ensured that they did control education and the appointment of personnel so as to build up a group of reliable supporters in key areas and ensure that future generations were educated in Communist principles.

Having gained popular support the Communist SED gradually eliminated other political groups and views.

- The Soviet military command suppressed political party activity in Berlin. CDU and LDPD activities were ended.
- Free expression was severely limited and political dissent was restrained.
- The military government determined appointments and dismissals.

Democracy was formally abandoned in 1948–9, and the SED announced a **Marxist-Leninist** 'Party of a New Type'. It was based on the principle of **democratic centralism**. It also established 'mass organisations' under Communist control of youth, women and unions in the Soviet zone.

The growing divisions between the zones

In 1947 economic problems resulted in the British and American zones being merged to form **Bizonia**. The French joined in 1949 to form **Trizonia**. Disputes developed over Soviet reparations from the Western zones. There were also growing divisions between Russia and the West over the **Truman Doctrine** and **Marshall Aid**.

A growing **black market** resulted in the introduction of the Deutschmark in the Western zones, but the Soviets refused to follow suit. They brought in their own currency, the East German mark.

Support or challenge?

Below is a question which asks you how far you agree with a specific statement. Below this are a series of general statements and sources which are relevant to the question. Using your own knowledge and the information on the pages 38 and 40, decide whether these statements and the sources support or challenge the statement in the question and tick the appropriate box.

'The Communists never intended the **GDR** to remain democratic.' How far do you agree with this statement?

	SUPPORT	CHALLENGE
Elections were to be held in Germany, starting at local level.		
A range of political parties were established in the Russian zone.		
Communists were to be in charge of Personnel Questions and Education.		
Not all mayors were Communists.		
All parties were brought together in a 'National Front'.		
Mass organisations were put under Communist control.		
Liberal and religious parties were allowed.		
Source A		
Source B		

SOURCE A

Ulbricht explains the early role of the Communists in Berlin.

The local government administration has to be put together correctly, as far as politics is concerned. We can't use Communists as Mayors … In working-class districts the mayors should be Social Democrats. It is obviously quite clear: it has to appear to be democratic, but we must keep everything under our control.

From Wolfgang Leonhard, who later defected to the West, *Die Revolution Entlasst Ihre Kinder*, published 1955

SOURCE B

The KPD founding declaration.

We are of the opinion that it would be wrong to impose the Soviet system forcibly upon Germany, because this path does not accord with the current conditions of development in Germany.

We are rather of the view that the decisive interests of the German people in the current situation prescribe a different path for Germany, and that is the path of establishing an anti-fascist, democratic regime, a parliamentary-democratic Republic with all the democratic rights and freedoms for the people.

At this historic turning point we Communists call to all working people, to all democratic and progressive forces among the people, to join this great struggle for the democratic renewal of Germany, for the rebirth of our land!

From Rolf Steininger, *Deutsche Geschichte Seit 1945*, published 1996

The Berlin Blockade and the emergence of the GDR

The Berlin Blockade

From 24 June 1948 to 12 May 1949 – as a result of growing divisions between the Western Allies and the Soviets, particularly over currency – the Soviets blocked access to West Berlin. They aimed to starve West Berlin, and force its merger into the Soviet zone.

The Allies supplied West Berlin by air and brought in food, medical supplies and fuel. This showed the Soviets they would not relinquish control of their zone. West Berlin became a symbol of resistance to the spread of communism and confirmed the division of Germany.

The division of Germany and the East German Constitution

In 1948 Western representatives met in the '**Parliamentary Council**' and devised a constitution for a Federal Republic (**FRG**). The German Democratic Republic (GDR) was formed from the Soviet zone in October 1949 with a new constitution.

The constitution declared the state temporary, awaiting reunification.

- The parliament – **Volkskammer** – claimed to represent the people. It was not democratically elected and the number of seats for each party was allocated before the election.
- The Upper House – **Länderkammer** – represented the five regions (this was abolished in 1958).
- The President – formal Head of State – was Wilhelm Pieck.
- The Prime Minister – head of government – was Otto Grotewohl.

However, power remained with the Communist Party's General Secretary (Ulbricht), **Politburo**, Central Committee and local party units.

A 'state within a state' was established with the creation of State Security Service (**Stasi**) in 1950 and was aided by the 'People's Police in Barracks' – regular police and border guards. There was greater surveillance and repression. **Länder** were abolished in 1952 and replaced with smaller units – **Bezirke** – which were easier for the party to control.

The 1953 Rising

Events

On 16 June, workers on the Stalinallee, a prestige building project, demanded an end to increased working hours for no more pay. They called a general strike, which became political as workers demanded the removal of Ulbricht and reunification with the West. Concerned about crushing the unrest and the unreliability of his own forces, Ulbricht called in Soviet troops. They dispersed the strikers, but unrest continued.

The causes

The rising was caused by a number of factors and was the culmination of long-term disquiet. The death of Stalin and the apparent promise of greater freedoms with the announcement of the '**New Course**' in the Soviet Union encouraged unrest. Ulbricht had already been summoned to Moscow and warned that his policies were causing disquiet because of:

- the tightening of border controls
- enforced **collectivisation** of agriculture
- government demands for increased productivity from workers, but without an increase in pay
- Ulbricht's policy of 'Building of Socialism', which was announced in 1952 and increased the role of the state
- the failure of the government to persuade people of the need for changes.

Consequences

- The increase in working hours was ended and more consumer goods were to be produced to improve living standards.
- The SED (The Communist Party) became more worried about potential unrest and adopted a harder line, increasing the powers and size of the Stasi.
- Ulbricht's power was strengthened.
- It became apparent that the West would not intervene to help.

Doing reliability well

Below are a series of definitions listing common reasons why sources are unreliable, and two sources. Under each source, explain why the source is either reliable or unreliable for the purpose stated, justifying your answer by referring to the following definitions.

- **Vested interest**: the source is written so that the writer can protect their power or financial interests.
- **Second-hand report**: the writer of the source is not an eyewitness, but is relying on someone else's account.
- **Expertise**: the source is written on a subject in which the author (for example, a historian) is an expert.
- **Political bias**: the source is written by a politician and it reflects their political views.
- **Reputation**: the source is written to protect the writer's reputation.

SOURCE A

The East German government comment on the unrest in Berlin in 1953.

Yesterday's decision on the question of norms has removed the cause of the cessation of work by the building workers in Berlin. The unrest which ensued is the work of agents provocateurs and fascist agents of foreign Powers and their accomplices from German capitalist monopolies. These forces are dissatisfied with the democratic power in the German Democratic Republic, which is organising improvements in the situation of the population. The Government appeals to the people.

Statement by the Government of the German Democratic Republic regarding the unrest in Berlin, 17 June 1953

The source is reliable/unreliable as an explanation of the causes of unrest in the GDR in 1953 because

_____

_____

_____

SOURCE B

The SED comment on the unrest of June 1953.

It is clear from a large number of party reports that, on publication of the communiqué, the majority of local party leaders and members were shocked, uncertain, and in the main helpless (the same story comes across in all reports, particularly from comrades working right at the grass roots) … The response on the part of party leaders and members is explicable by the fact that, in recent weeks, many comrades have had a hard time trying to defend and justify the [previous] resolutions (travel costs, foodstuffs, prices, etc), in often stormy confrontations … It is often suggested that the party has isolated itself from the masses, that too many rose-coloured reports had been given to the top party leadership and that the latter was therefore unaware of the real mood among the population …

An Internal SED report on the unrest of 1953

The source is reliable/unreliable as an explanation of the causes of unrest in the GDR in 1953 because

_____

_____

_____

Economic change in the GDR

Land reform

Large estates had been given to peasants in 1945, but this created problems. They were unable to farm profitably, as they lacked resources and machinery. In 1952 the SED introduced collectivisation and formed 'land production co-operatives' (LPGs) as part of the plan for the 'Building of Socialism'. Mechanisation and the use of tractor-lending stations became possible, making agriculture more efficient. The policy was not popular with many, who abandoned their farms and fled to the West. This caused food shortages and a drop in production levels, which contributed to unrest in 1953.

By 1959 LPGs made up 45 per cent of the agricultural sector. By 1961 this figure was 85 per cent, but production had decreased further and rationing returned. This resulted in more people leaving, and was a major reason for the building of the **Berlin Wall**.

Industry and nationalisation

The 1950s

During occupation, many large industries were placed under state ownership (nationalised). Most people worked in 'People's Own Factories' (***Volkseigene Betriebe***/VEBs), owned and managed by the state. The party set targets, handled discipline and ran social activities, all of which increased their control.

The emphasis was on heavy industry. Production targets, which were often unrealistic, were set in **Five Year Plans**, which were often changed and increased.

There was some up-turn in the economy at the end of the 1950s.

Problems with the Five Year Plans

- Targets ignored consumer demands.
- Emphasis on quantity over quality reduced saleability.
- Plans were often out of date before they were implemented.
- Prices were fixed, but did not link to supply and demand.

Living standards improved slowly compared to the FRG. A metal worker earned less than 300 marks per month, whereas a manager earned 4000 or even 15,000. Managers also received perks such as cheap mortgages and separate canteens, all of which caused disquiet.

The Seven Year Plan

In 1959 a **Seven Year Plan** was implemented to align economic development of the GDR with the Soviet Union. This plan brought in some consumer goods and improvements in living and working conditions. However, the consumer goods were expensive and not made in large enough quantities. Rationing did not end until 1958, another reason why many left for the West.

The 1960s

The Berlin Wall stabilised the workforce as there was less movement to the West and resulted in some economic freedoms as there was less fear of losing workers. In 1962 the Seven Year Plan was abandoned because of economic problems. A new plan for 1962–70 was drawn up, but never implemented.

However, a 'New Economic System for Planning and Direction' (NOSPL) was introduced in 1963, which:

- brought more flexibility and input from workers
- allowed workers to share in profits, which encouraged production
- emphasised quality rather than quantity.

These developments encouraged social change as the middle class left, often to go to the West.

Add own knowledge

Below are a question and Sources A–C. In one colour, draw links between the sources to show ways in which they agree about the success of agricultural policies in the GDR. In another colour, draw links between the sources to show ways in which they disagree. Around the edge of the sources, write relevant own knowledge. Again, draw links to show the ways in which this agrees and disagrees with the sources.

Do you agree with the view that the agricultural policies of the GDR were a success? Explain your answer, using Sources A–C and your own knowledge.

SOURCE A

The government in the Eastern zone announces land reform.

The Land Reform must guarantee the liquidation of large estates held by feudal Junkers and must put an end to the rule of Junkers and large estate owners on the villages because this has always been a bastion of reaction and of fascism in our country and was one of the main sources of aggression and of the wars of conquest against other peoples. The Land Reform is to fulfil the perennial dream of the landless and land-hungry peasants and agricultural labourers that the large estates should pass into their hands … Landed property in our German homeland must be based on firm, healthy and productive peasant holdings which are the private property of their occupants.

An extract from a decree on land reform in Saxony, 1945

SOURCE B

A Protestant Bishop writes to the Prime Minister of the GDR about the impact of collectivisation.

In view of certain measures and methods in the course of the socialisation of agriculture, and out of a concern for people living in rural areas, we see it as our duty to bring the following matters to your attention. It is not a matter for the Church to take decisions with respect to economic questions concerning socialisation. But such shattering news is constantly coming to us from our pastors and parishes with respect to the methods being used to get individual farmers to enter into agricultural production co-operatives. It would go too far to describe these methods in detail. But it is a fact that farmers are being forced against their will to enter into agricultural production co-operatives, using economic, political and moral pressures, and with the involvement of state lawyers, police, and the organs of the State Security Service; and that they are then being forced to declare in writing that this occurred 'voluntarily'.

An extract from a letter from a Protestant Bishop to the Prime Minister of the GDR, March 1960

SOURCE C

A modern historian comments on the impact of agricultural changes in the GDR.

A first wave of collectivisation took place in 1952, coinciding with the 'building of socialism'. This was sufficiently unpopular that many farmers preferred simply to abandon their farms and flee west, while there was still the opportunity. Resulting problems with food supply to the towns contributed to the widespread social unrest of 1953. A second great wave of collectivisation in 1960–1 also precipitated mass flight.

From Mary Fulbrook, *Democracy and Dictatorship in Germany 1919–1963*, 2008

Social change in the GDR

There were opportunities for those who committed themselves to the new political system. Those who gained the most were peasants, the working class and women.

Peasants

- Gained land, but were later forced to join a collective.
- Better machinery to work the farms.
- Opportunity of education.

Factory workers

- Opportunity of education.
- Opportunity to manage factories if they were loyal to the party.

Women

- Many became doctors.
- Increased support with the provision of maternity care, crèches and after-school facilities to allow women to work part-time or at lower levels.

Mass organisations

The state established a number of mass organisations to give them control of all aspects of life. They included:

- Free German Trade Union League (FDGB) – established for workers, but the SED controlled its policies
- the Democratic Women's League of Germany – the mass organisation for women
- the League of Culture – had the support of many intellectuals who wanted to establish an anti-fascist state
- the Society for Sport and Technology – organised sporting opportunities, but was also a preparation for military service
- the German–Soviet Friendship Society – attempted to improve relations with Russia, and reinforced the idea that the Soviets had liberated Germany from fascism.

Youth education

The youth were the future, and needed to be won over to Communist views. Schools became comprehensive 'polytechnic' schools, with close links to industry or sport, and provided practical work experience. The SED controlled youth organisations.

Scholarships were available for the disadvantaged, and university was opened up to all. Those from professional and aristocratic classes were often discriminated against. Many left to study in the West.

Youth opposition

Not all were won over by state views. There was some support for Western culture, based around rock and roll music. The state response varied from clampdowns to tolerance.

Religion and the Churches

East German society was still religious. There were 15 million Protestants and 1 million Catholics. The SED wanted religion to wither away and fulfil **Karl Marx's** prophecy that it was only the 'opiate of the people'. At first the Church avoided the changes brought in by the SED:

- Church-owned land was not seized.
- Ministers were not de-Nazified or removed from office.
- Churches ran their own internal affairs.

The situation changed in 1946 with the Law for the Democratisation of German Schools. This removed religious education from the curriculum. In 1952–3 there was a state campaign against Junge Gemeinde, the Protestant Youth Group. Members were prevented from remaining at school, taking their final exams and going to university. The campaign ended in June 1953.

Jugendweihe

In 1954 the Youth Dedication Service (*Jugendweihe*) was imposed on the young. This involved a commitment to Marxist views. As these contradicted Christian views the service caused conflict. However, refusal resulted in discrimination at school and prevented post-compulsory education or a professional career. Churches were forced to change their view and accept that the Dedication did not contradict Christian confirmation. This forced them into a relationship with the atheist state.

Explain the difference

The following sources give different accounts of the impact of Communist rule on people in the GDR.
List the ways in which the sources differ. Explain the difference between the sources using the provenance
of the sources alone.

SOURCE A

A physician who sought refuge in West Berlin describes conditions prevailing in the Aue uranium mines in Eastern Germany.

The refugee physician, who had a practice at Aue, stated that of about 300,000 men employed in the area, 200,000 suffered from venereal disease. He ascribed this to the forced influx of thousands of young workers into an environment where they lived separated from their families, ill-treated, and with little prospect of any change in their position. Neither the Russians nor the East German authorities seemed interested in meeting the problem. A further tragedy was the number of illegitimate children who were born diseased and suffered from malnutrition and for whom no one cared. To the inhabitants of Aue they are known as 'the rats'.

The physician stated that he had tried to keep a home going for these foundlings, and to encourage the opening of foster homes, but his efforts had been constantly thwarted by the authorities. The miners themselves were recruited by threats and pressure, and many were youths who refused to serve in the police. They lived in overcrowded hutments surrounded by barbed wire.

The Times, 8 May 1953

SOURCE B

From an interview with a woman born in 1931, carried out for a research project on generations in the GDR.

I experienced the end of the war as a thirteen-year-old in the former East Prussia with all the horrors of the Second World War. Expulsion in 1947 out of homeland [Heimat]. Resettling [Übersiedlung] with very ill mother into the former GDR. Father died after being transported in April 1945 to Siberia. Then as a seventeen-year-old, all alone and without any means of support, survived a very difficult time. After marriage in 1951 and the birth of a son a new life began. We were happy and also contented with our life.

Mary Fulbrook (ed.), *Power and Society in the GDR*, 2008

Develop the detail

Below are a question and a paragraph written in answer to this question. The paragraph contains a limited amount of detail. Annotate the paragraph to add additional detail to the answer.

To what extent did Communist rule bring about changes in East German society?

The advent of Communist rule brought about increased opportunities for many groups in East German society who supported Communist rule. Loyal workers had increased social and economic opportunities and women were also able to play an increased role in society due to social provisions. The same was true of children from working class backgrounds as educational opportunities were provided for them. However, these gains must be balanced against the control the party had over individuals through mass organisations, which controlled a wide range of aspects of life.

The Berlin Wall

In the 1950s, many travelled from East to West Berlin. This increased in 1956 when the **Hungarian Uprising** was crushed. Many left the East to escape repression.

In 1958, **Khrushchev** demanded that the Western powers recognise the GDR, withdraw from West Berlin and hand over access routes. The Soviets wanted to force the West to recognise the East German state, but the Allies ignored his threat.

The USA had poured large amounts of aid into West Berlin and, in comparison, East Berlin was not prosperous. Many left the East for West Berlin, including skilled and qualified workers attracted to its freedom, cinemas, shops and better standard of living. The Communists saw it as 'capitalist infection'. This exodus had a severe impact on the economy of the East as well as undermining communism.

Year	Number who left East Germany	Year	Number who left East Germany
1949	129,245	1956	279,189
1950	197,788	1957	261,622
1951	165,648	1958	204,092
1952	182,393	1959	143,917
1953	331,390	1960	199,188
1954	184,198	1961	159,730
1955	252,870	Total	2,691,270

The number of people who left East Germany 1949–61

The events of 1961

June
The Vienna Summit. Khrushchev pressurised US President Kennedy to withdraw Western forces from West Berlin within six months. Although inexperienced, Kennedy promised to protect freedom in West Berlin.

July 17
The West rejected Khrushchev's demands.

July 23
The East imposed strict travel restrictions. Up to 1000 refugees had been leaving each day.

July 25
Kennedy gave a further guarantee to West Berlin, and announced increased arms spending.

August 13
A barbed-wire barrier along the border between East and West Berlin was erected by East German soldiers, which ended free movement.

August 22
Barbed-wire was replaced by a concrete wall. All routes to the West were closed, except Checkpoint Charlie.

October
US diplomats and troops crossed into the East, to test the Soviet reaction.

October 27
Soviet tanks arrived at Checkpoint Charlie and refused to allow access to East Berlin. However, after this there was a gradual pull back of forces.

Consequences of the Berlin Wall

- Berlin was divided physically. Free access to the West was ended and families were divided.
- An exodus of workers was prevented. Those caught attempting to escape were shot.
- The workforce in the East was stabilised and economic progress in the East improved.
- The East introduced limited liberalisation and decentralisation to win the support of the population.
- The Four-Power agreement on Berlin was ended.
- Kennedy refused proposals to pull down the Wall, and appeared weak.
- Khrushchev failed to remove the West from Berlin, and appeared weak.
- Increased tensions between the East and West, which encouraged the development of nuclear weapons.
- **Propaganda** for the West – why did the East have to stop people escaping?

Conclusion: What was the situation in East Germany at the end of the period?

- A **totalitarian** dictatorship had been established.
- Ulbricht, a hard-line **Stalinist**, had not followed the **de-Stalinisation** policies of the USSR.
- Ulbricht attempted to bring about **social justice**.
- Force and violence were not a regular part of life. They were seen more at the start and end of the period.

Explain the difference

Sources A and B below give different reasons for the building of the Berlin Wall. List the ways in which the sources differ. Explain the differences between the sources using the provenance of the sources alone.

SOURCE A

The Americans explain why they believe the Wall was built.

By the very admission of the East German authorities, the measures which have just been taken are motivated by the fact that an ever-increasing number of inhabitants of East Germany wish to leave this territory. The reasons for this exodus are known. They are simply the internal difficulties in East Germany.

An extract from a United States note to the USSR on the Berlin Wall, 17 August 1961

SOURCE B

The East German leader Walter Ulbricht implies his aims for West Berlin.

Ulbricht said that no one could fly over or enter East German national territory without a visa from East Germany. Such visas would not be given to 'undesirables'. Foreign airlines would not be allowed to overfly the East German territory without a special agreement. He did not think that Tempelhof [in West Berlin] would be a suitable airport for Berlin, but if its use was continued there would have to be East German control there.

Extract from a report to the British Prime Minister Harold Macmillan after two Conservative MPs met Ulbricht at the Leipzig Trade Fair, East Germany, September 1961

Doing reliability well

Below are a series of definitions listing common reasons why sources are unreliable. On page 50 are three sources. Under each source, explain why the source is either reliable or unreliable for the purpose stated, justifying your answer by referring to the following definitions.

- **Vested interest**: the source is written so that the writer can protect their power or financial interests.
- **Second-hand report**: the writer of the source is not an eyewitness, but is relying on someone else's account.
- **Expertise**: the source is written on a subject in which the author (for example, a historian) is an expert.
- **Political bias**: the source is written by a politician and reflects their political views.
- **Reputation**: the source is written to protect the writer's reputation.

SOURCE A

A former West Berliner describes in his memoirs how easy it was for those from the West to buy cheap goods in East Berlin in the late 1950s.

For a Westerner, a beer in a pub in East Berlin cost just a quarter or a third of what you had to pay in the West. We Westerners could visit a hairdresser for a few coins. For a handful of change we could spend an evening at the State Opera in East Berlin, or the Berliner Ensemble Theatre. For next to nothing we could go into state-owned stores and buy records or books. East Berlin was a shopping paradise, a kind of duty-free port. The only thing was, you mustn't let yourself be caught with these low-priced goods on your way back into West Berlin.

Joachim Trenkner, *Coca Cola schmecks nach Berlin*, 2004

The source is reliable/unreliable as evidence of the reasons for the closing of the frontier with West Berlin because

_____

_____

SOURCE B

The East Germans explain the reasons for the closing of the border with West Berlin.

To stop hostile activities by those who want revenge and to conquer us and also by militaristic forces in West Germany and West Berlin, a border control will be introduced at the borders to the GDR, including the border with the western sectors of Greater Berlin, as is common on the borders of sovereign states. Borders to West Berlin will be sufficiently guarded and effectively controlled in order to prevent subversive activities from the West.

An extract from the Resolution of the GDR Council of Ministers, 12 August 1961

The source is reliable/unreliable as evidence of the reasons for the closing of the frontier with West Berlin because

_____

_____

SOURCE C

The West German Chancellor comments on the closing of the border.

Your sorrow and suffering are our sorrow and suffering. In your particularly difficult situation you were able to at least derive some comfort from the thought that, if your lot should become quite unbearable, you could mend it by fleeing. Now it looks as if you have been deprived of that comfort, too, for reasons which have no justification in reality.

Adenauer's message to East Germans after the closing of the frontier in Berlin. This message was part of a speech to a specially called meeting of the German parliament, 18 August, 1961

The source is reliable/unreliable as evidence of the reasons for the closing of the frontier with West Berlin because

_____

_____

Exam focus

On pages 52–3 is a sample A-grade answer to the exam-style question below. Read the answer and the examiner comments around it. You could try answering the question below first before looking at the sample answer.

Compare these sources as evidence for the reasons for the building of the Berlin Wall in 1961.

SOURCE A

The East German leader Walter Ulbricht justifies the building of the Berlin Wall.

This is an anti-fascist protection wall. Counter-revolutionary vermin, spies, profiteers, human traffickers, prostitutes, spoiled teenage hooligans and other enemies of the people's democratic order have been sucking on our workers' and peasants' Republic like leeches and bugs on a healthy body. Naturally they would have liked to continue sucking the blood and life force from our people, but if one does not combat the weeds they will smother the young seed. This is why we have sealed the cracks in the fabric of our house through which the worst enemies of the German people could creep.

From an article in the East German newspaper, *Neues Deutschland*, August 1961

SOURCE B

A Soviet newspaper gives an explanation for the building of the Berlin Wall.

The Western powers in Berlin use it as a centre of subversive activity against the GDR. In no other part of the world are so many centres of espionage to be found. These centres smuggle their agents into the GDR for all kinds of subversion: recruiting spies, sabotage, provoking disturbances. The government presents all working people of the GDR with a proposal that will securely block subversive activity so that reliable safeguards and effective control will be established around West Berlin, including its border with democratic East Berlin.

From *Isvestia*, a Soviet newspaper, October 1961

Compare these sources as evidence for the reasons for the building of the Berlin Wall in 1961.

The candidate gives a very clear overview of the arguments of the two sources about the issue in the question, suggesting that their general view is similar. It is a good idea to start with a direct comparison of the overall view of the two sources, even if you then acknowledge that there are some differences.

The answer starts to go beyond the overview and acknowledges that the emphasis of the two sources is different and this is developed in the subsequent lines.

The answer uses provenance to explain the reasons offered for the building, integrating content and provenance. The points are fully developed and explained. Rather than simply asserting that both sources are propaganda, the answer explains how they are used to justify the building.

The focus is on the origin and although this makes the reliability of both sources questionable, the latter part of the discussion of both sources shows a very good understanding of the possible hidden message of Eastern and Communist fears.

Both sources argue that the West and its policies were to blame for the building of the Berlin Wall and therefore see it as a defensive measure. Both sources are from just after the building of the Wall and see it as a necessary response to Western attempts to undermine the GDR through an aggressive policy of external and internal subversion; however the emphasis in the two sources is different. The focus of Source A is much wider than that of Source B; Source A, written by the East German leader, focuses on the West's attempts to undermine the GDR politically, economically and socially because he would be concerned about the supposed and serious impact of the West on his country and more specifically East Berlin, whereas Source B, from the Soviet Union, focuses on the traditional and wider Cold War agenda and issues of spies, espionage and saboteurs. Both sources are clear attempts by the GDR and the Soviets to justify the building of the Wall, limiting their value as reliable evidence for the building, but providing typical Communist justifications. Ulbricht's use of emotive and exaggerated language in Source A, portraying the West as fascist and using the images of the West as leeches and low life, 'sucking the blood' from 'a healthy body', is a more emotive attempt at justification. On the other hand, Source B is more reasoned in its tone. Ulbricht's tone is more exaggerated and fearful because his audience was his own people and therefore he wants to portray the threat, and hence the justification, as more immediate and direct, hence the images of 'human traffickers, prostitutes and spoiled teenage hooligans', but he was also more concerned than the Soviet Union by the exodus of skilled workers to the West and this may explain the exaggeration and portrayal of the corrupt Western lifestyle which is bringing crime and sleaze to the East. However, Source B's concerns are much wider and see the building of the Wall as helping to bring security to all 'working people'.

As both sources are Communist, the reliability of both, in terms of their explanation for the building of the Wall, must be questioned. They are both from a heavily controlled and censored press, and it is likely that there was some collaboration between Moscow and East Berlin about comments justifying the building of the Wall. As Source A was written by the East German leader he is unlikely to be critical of his own nation, although it could be argued that his references subtly acknowledge the successful penetration of East Berlin by the West, which enabled them to 'suck the life force from the people' and attract the East German workers, particularly skilled, to the West and therefore the Wall was needed to prevent this exodus. Source B might also acknowledge that East Germany faced some problems and needed the Wall to control its people; the reference to 'provoking disturbances' might be a reference to the 1953 unrest. Therefore both sources may hint at possible internal reasons for the building of the Wall, but try to hide the need to deal with these behind an attack on Western policy towards Berlin and communism in general.

The usefulness of both sources in explaining the reasons for the building of the Wall is limited as they both take a standard Communist propaganda line, but they are useful in terms of the rhetoric that was used to justify the building, and behind some of the attacks on the West there are hints of the concerns that the East genuinely had. It might be argued that Source B is more useful as the espionage mentioned was a reality during the Cold War, although Source A, coming from the leader of East Germany and specifically aimed at an East German audience, is useful in outlining his and his government's concerns.

Although the conclusion suggests that both sources have both limitations and value, it is not a case of the answer 'sitting on the fence'; the judgement is justified and explained and therefore this is a valid conclusion.

28/30

The answer consistently focuses on the demands of the question, with direct comparison of the two sources made throughout. There is a good balance between the content of the sources and their provenance. The answer deals with a range of issues concerning provenance, focusing on the key issues of tone and purpose. A clear judgement is reached about the usefulness of the sources and this is clearly linked to the actual question of the reasons for the building of the Berlin Wall, rather than a general answer about the usefulness of the sources. The answer also picks up on a number of subtleties, such as the possible Communist concern with the loss of workers and therefore the admission that it was not just a response to Western aggression, which might be expected in sources of this type. The use of brief references to the actual content of the passage is good as the answer avoids the common mistake of copying out large sections that obscure the argument. The answer is also successful at integrating the content and provenance and also avoiding the excessive use of own knowledge, but where it is used, as in the reference to the 1953 Rising, it is both useful and brief. The answer deals with all the main issues raised and provides a balanced evaluation of the content and provenance; as a result the answer was awarded Level 1a and would score virtually full marks.

Understanding the demands of the question

In different colours, underline examples where the answer directly compares the content of the two passages and where it directly compares the provenance in order to explain the similarities and differences between the two passages.

Section 4:
How far did Western democratic structures succeed in the Federal Republic?

At Yalta and Potsdam, the Allies had agreed to keep a single state, yet they had different concepts of its social, economic and political organisation.

Problems in the Western zone

Germany suffered total defeat in 1945, with occupation and massive territorial losses. Following its surrender Germany ceased to exist as a state and had to be administered by the Allies. There were three Western zones – British, French and American – and this was repeated for Berlin. The Allied Control Council (ACC) was the military governing body whose decisions had to be unanimous, and when this failed each military governor could implement decisions in their zone, which resulted in different policies in each zone.

There were severe economic problems which could better be addressed by greater co-operation between the zones.

Problems following the Second World War:

- food and fuel shortages
- homelessness
- bereavement
- integration into civilian society was problematic for soldiers
- refugees
- dealing with the impact of **genocide**
- the collapse of the currency.

Events in the Western zone

The timeline below outlines the developments towards greater unity within the Western zone:

1946
The USA drew up plans for German reconstruction, but Russia and France did not agree. France did not want a strong Germany and wanted large **reparations**; it even annexed the **Saar** for a short period.

1946–7
A severe winter worsened conditions. A weak British economy, with bread rationing at home, meant it was unable to fund its zone.

1947
By 1947 economic recovery was essential to prevent an economic crisis and social revolution in Western Europe. Food had to be imported, which cost $700 million per year. The problem was made worse as some industry had been dismantled to pay reparations and there had been an influx of refugees. The British and American zones were merged to form **Bizonia**. Aid was poured into the Western zone.

1948
The **Marshall Plan** was applied to the Western zone. The **London Conference**, between February and June 1948, agreed a West German currency and state. From summer 1948 onwards, Western representatives of the '**Parliamentary Council**' started to devise a constitution for a new state in the West.

1949
France, after initial resistance, joined and created **Trizonia**. A new constitution, the **Basic Law**, was adopted in May 1949, which established a West German state.

East–West tensions

Developments in the West resulted in divergence from the East. A **black market** had grown in the West due to the weakness of the currency and the introduction of a new currency, the Deutschmark, was essential before aid was brought in. This antagonised the USSR and resulted in the Berlin Blockade, which confirmed the division of Germany.

Russia stated that 'technical difficulties' – the reason given by the Russians for the blockade – would continue until plans for a West German government were abandoned.

Support or challenge?

Below is a question which asks you how far you agree with a specific statement. Below this is a series of general statements which are relevant to the question. Using your own knowledge and the information on the opposite page, decide whether these statements support or challenge the statement in the question and tick the appropriate box.

'Economic difficulties were the most serious problem in the Western zones.' How far do you agree with this statement?

	SUPPORT	CHALLENGE
There were severe food and fuel shortages in the Western zone.		
There had been a large influx of refugees from the East.		
The Western zone had suffered large-scale damage during the war.		
The new government had to overcome the impact of Nazi rule and genocide.		
The structure of the ACC and the need to achieve unanimous decisions created difficulties.		
There were divisions between France, USA and Great Britain.		
The weakness of the British economy meant they were unable to support their zone.		
The weakness of the German currency and the resultant black market created economic problems.		
Inflation severely damaged the economy in the Western zone.		

Spot the inference

High level answers avoid summarising or paraphrasing the sources, and instead make inferences from the sources. Below are a source and a series of statements. Read the source and decide which of the statements:

- make an inference from the source (I)
- paraphrase the source (P)
- summarise the source (S)
- cannot be justified from the source (X).

SOURCE A

The American Secretary of State explains the need for German economic unity.

The United States is firmly of the belief that Germany should be administered as an economic unit and that zonal barriers should be completely obliterated so far as economic life and activity in Germany are concerned. The conditions which now exist in Germany make it impossible for industrial production to reach the levels which the occupying powers agreed were essential for a minimum German economy. Obviously, if the agreed levels of industry are to be reached, we cannot continue to restrict the free exchange of commodities throughout Germany. The time has come when the zonal boundaries should be regarded as defining only the areas to be occupied for security purposes by the armed forces of the occupying powers, and not as self-contained economic or political units.

An extract from James Byrnes' Stuttgart speech of September 1946

Statement	I	P	S	X
Conditions within Germany were bad.				
Russia was the main obstacle to German recovery.				
The USA wanted to unite Germany.				
The USA wanted greater economic unity.				
The USA wanted Germany to be able to recover economically.				
Economic prosperity was needed for German recovery.				
There were tensions among the wartime Allies.				
Economic barriers were hindering Germany reaching the targets agreed.				

The West German constitution

Revised

In May 1949 a new constitution, the Basic Law, was adopted and in August 1949 Adenauer, leader of the Christian Democrats, was elected **Chancellor**.

The main features of the Basic Law were:

- Freedom of expression, assembly, association and movement were guaranteed.

- It established a 'representative' democracy whereby popular participation was limited to voting every few years and the public merely select who will rule for them. This kept power in the hands of the elite to prevent the emergence of another Hitler.

- Federal State: Individual states kept much power over regional issues, and at a national level they were represented in the Upper Chamber (**Bundesrat**).

- The Lower Chamber (**Bundestag**) was elected by a complex system which combined **proportional representation** with **first past the post**. It was later added that parties had to gain 5 per cent of the vote before they were represented. This was done to prevent the emergence of small, extremist parties.

- The Law was to be temporary until Germany was united. It committed Germany to work for unity and all Germans living in former German lands were allowed citizenship. All those who left the **GDR** were able to settle and work in the West.

- All parties had to uphold democracy. Extremist parties that were not committed to parliamentary democracy were banned. This prevented anti-democratic parties achieving a majority.

- The **President** was not directly elected, but was chosen by a representative convention. This prevented an anti-democratic leader. The powers of the President were limited, largely formal and symbolic, and prevented rule by decree.

- The Chancellor was appointed by the President, but needed parliamentary approval. The Chancellor could not be dismissed unless a new Chancellor was voted in, which prevented the President from appointing and dismissing a Chancellor at will. The proposed Chancellor had to have parliamentary support; if not new elections had to be called.

At first there were many small parties in West Germany, but gradually the numbers declined. This was because:

- The constitution banned far right and left parties.

- From 1953 the 5 per cent hurdle at federal level prevented smaller parties from gaining representation in the Bundestag. In 1957 the number of constituencies that had to be won was raised from one to three.

- Small parties were divided.

- Many right-wing groups joined the CDU (see page 58).

- Economic developments and prosperity were associated with the CDU (see page 60).

- Social changes (see page 64).

De-Nazification

There was a mass internment of former Nazis who had political responsibilities and leadership roles. The Allies wanted to remove Nazis from all positions in society, but it proved to be impracticable. Therefore in 1946 they decided to deal with **de-Nazification** on a case-by-case basis. Penalties were harsh and resulted in people playing down their Nazi past. Some obtained **affidavits** to show they were clear. It did not help Germany confront the past. When the German authorities took over the role many escaped punishment, some because they were useful in an anti-Communist role.

Mind map

Make a copy of the mind map below and use the information on the opposite page to add detail to it.

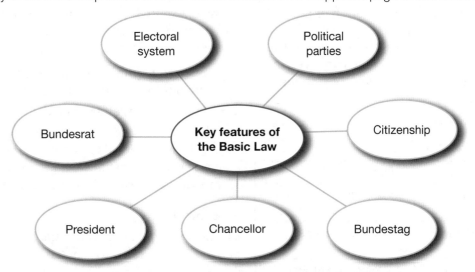

Develop the detail

(a)

Below are a question and a paragraph written in answer to this question. The paragraph contains a limited amount of detail. Annotate the paragraph to add additional detail to the answer.

'The main aim of the Basic Law was to prevent democracy from being undermined by constitutional means.' How far do you agree?

There were many elements of the Basic Law that were designed to prevent a repeat of 1932–3. Political parties had to support the system and those that did not were banned. The President was not voted for by the people and his powers were limited. The Chancellor had to be approved by parliament and could not be simply dismissed by the President. The voting system was designed to prevent small parties from being represented and the combination of two electoral systems also ensured that more extreme parties were unlikely to gain seats.

Spectrum of significance

Below are a question and a list of general points which could be used to answer the question. Use your own knowledge and the information on pages 56, 58, 60 and 62 to reach a judgement about the importance of these general points to the question posed. Write numbers on the spectrum below to indicate their relative importance. Having done this, write a brief justification of your placement, explaining why some of these factors are more important than others. The resulting diagram could form the basis of an essay plan.

How far do you agree that the constitution was the main reason for the disappearance of a multi-party system in West Germany?

1. Broad-based appeal of Adenauer's CDU.
2. Splits within the smaller parties.
3. The banning of extremist and non-democratic parties.
4. The electoral safeguards, including the 5 per cent hurdle.
5. The economic success.
6. Adenauer's international success.

←──→

Most important factor   Least important factor

Political parties

In 1945 the Allies allowed the formation of political parties, and four major parties and some smaller ones emerged. By 1949 politics was dominated by two main parties: the CDU and SPD. However, the FDP often held the balance of power, even though it was a small party.

The table below shows the political parties in West Germany in 1949.

Party	Beliefs
Christian Democrats (CDU/CSU)	Conservative
Social Democratic Party (SPD)	Democratic-socialist
Free Democratic Party (FDP)	Amalgamation of liberal parties
German Party (DP)	Right-wing
League of Refugees and Expellees (BHE)	Revisionist, nationalist, special-interest
Communist (KPD)	Communist: banned in 1956
Socialist Reich Party (SRP)	Pro-Nazi: banned in 1952

The SPD and KPD were established quickly. The Christian and Conservative Parties joined to form the CDU (Christian Democratic Union), although in Bavaria it was the Christian Social Union (CSU). The liberal parties formed the Free Democratic Party (FDP), which had liberal principles and business interests but also some right-wing views.

The CDU

The Christian Democrats were conservative Christians who had previously been members of the Catholic Centre Party or Protestant parties. Many had been conservative nationalists under Weimar and some were former Nazis. They:

- supported **capitalism** and competition but also wanted to protect the vulnerable
- supported the **welfare state**
- followed the Ahlen Programme, which outlined beliefs in traditional Christian values, a social conscience and the free market. However, in 1957 this was replaced with centre-conservative policies.

The SPD

The Social Democrats were a traditional socialist party. They appealed to workers. They:

- had been formed from Marxist and working class-movements
- abandoned Marxism in 1959 at the Bad Godesberg Conference
- wanted social justice combined with individual freedom.

Elections and election results

From 1949 to 1963 Konrad Adenauer was Chancellor of Germany and presided over a series of **coalition** governments. Because of his control and power over his own government ministers, his period in power is often referred to as **Chancellor Democracy**. It was also a period when elections were little more than a series of **plebiscites** in favour of the government. It has been argued that it removed popular self-government. However, it did ensure a responsible government.

	CDU/CSU		SPD		FDP		KPD		Others	
Year	%	seats	%	seats	%	seats	%	seats	%	seats
1949	31	139	29.2	131	11.9	52	5.7	15	22.2	65
1953	45.2	243	28.8	151	9.5	48	2.2	0	14.3	45
1957	50.2	270	31.8	169	7.7	41	–	–	10.3	17
1961	45.3	242	36.2	190	12.8	67	–	–	5.7	0

Table showing election results in the FRG

Explain the difference

The following sources give different accounts of reactions to the construction of the **Berlin Wall**. List the ways in which the sources differ. Explain the differences between the sources using the provenance of the sources alone.

SOURCE A

An aide to the Chancellor remembers Adenauer's reaction to the building of the Wall and its impact on the election campaign.

It was obvious from the beginning that the Chancellor had decided to play down the event as far as possible. 'Many recommend keeping quiet, and no sparks should fly into the powder keg! No-one did anything. Everything was running smoothly. Even from the top it was being said: remain calm in the Zone, remain calm in the West. The watchword was: the citizen's first duty is to remain calm.'

… Public reaction taught Adenauer that he had made three mistakes at one and the same time. Instead of expressing national solidarity in view of the emotional situation, as was expected of him, he continued the election campaign, while Brandt immediately cancelled his election campaign commitments. Instead of just going to the aid of Brandt and the Berliners in a paternal manner – the debate could be continued later – Adenauer polarised the election campaign. And he attacked his opponent not only politically but personally.

Hans Globke, a leading civil servant, recalls the events of 13 August 1961

SOURCE B

A Social Democrat outlines his hopes and policy for the future of Germany.

'I have said that the Wall is a sign of weakness. One could also say that it was a sign of fear and of the need for self-protection on the part of the Communist regime. The question arises as to whether there might be the possibility of gradually reducing these altogether justifiable concerns on the part of the regime, so that the relaxation of the borders and of the Wall will become practicable because the risk is bearable. That is a policy which could be summarised in the formula: change through rapprochement. I am firmly convinced that we can have enough self-confidence to follow such a policy without any illusions, which, quite apart from anything else, also fits seamlessly into the Western conception of a strategy for peace, since otherwise we would have to wait for a miracle, and that is no policy at all.'

Egon Bahr, speaking at the Protestant Academy in Tutzing, 15 July 1963

 ## How useful is a source?

Sources A and B above explained two different reactions to the building of the Berlin Wall. Look carefully at the statements in the table below and for each one decide which source is more useful in responding to the statement and explain your choice.

Statement	Source and explanation
The government mishandled the building of the Berlin Wall.	
Political parties in West Germany tried to exploit the building of the wall to their advantage.	
There were fears that the building of the wall would increase East–West tensions.	
Government policy towards the East was not supported by everyone.	
The building of the wall had little impact on West German politics.	

The Western economy

Food production in 1947 was only 51 per cent of 1938, and industrial output only 33 per cent. Initially the Allies prevented the rebuilding of the German economy and even dismantled the German steel industry. Reparations took away $10 billion, which damaged the economy further.

However, there was a gradual realisation that unless the West German economy recovered, the European economy could not recover and, in the 1950s, there was what has been described as an '**economic miracle**'.

Industrial production rose (see table below) resulting in higher wages; incomes went up 400 per cent between 1949 and 1963. Growth rates for GNP were about 8 per cent in the 1950s. Meanwhile, unemployment fell from 8.1 per cent (2 million) in 1950 to 0.5 per cent in 1965.

Why was there an 'economic miracle' in the West?

Recovery started with the creation of Bizonia in 1947 and with economic policies introduced before 1949 such as:

- removing price controls – this stimulated business by allowing free competition between private enterprises
- removing controls over wages and production – allowing workers a role in management and decision-making, which resulted in fewer strikes
- ending inflation through currency reform
- reducing marginal tax rates so that those on higher incomes had more money to spend on goods as higher rates of tax were reduced.

These policies encouraged people to work and were reflected in a decline in absenteeism as a work incentive had been provided. In Bizonia the index for industrial production had risen from 51 per cent in June 1948 to 78 per cent by December.

The West also had a number of advantages as it contained raw materials, had not suffered as much damage in the war as was feared and not as many reparations were taken as in the East. The work ethic of the population and availability of cheap labour from the East also meant they could meet the demands of the occupying forces.

Further stimulus was provided by Marshall Aid, although historians now question its importance. It had brought in only $2 billion by October 1954, and in 1948–9 provided less than 5 per cent of German national income. The Germans were also paying reparations and restitution payments to the Allies.

The **Korean War** (1950–3) increased the demand for goods the **Ruhr** could supply. This was helped by the fact other nations were unable to supply war materials, with the result that exports doubled.

Government policies may also have helped, although historians disagree on this. Dr Ludwig Erhard developed the 'social market economy' combining government legislation and a capitalism to produce 'prosperity for all'.

The economic recovery helped to provide political stability. As a result, Adenauer remained in power from 1949 until his resignation in 1963.

Year	All Industry	Mining	Consumer goods	Food
1951	109.6	107.2	108	113.8
1952	114.2	112.4	110.8	121.4
1953	122.1	114.8	118.9	124.6
1954	132.4	118.6	128	134.2
1955	138.3	126.9	138	145
1956	144.5	132.1	144.7	150.5
1957	155.1	138.9	157.4	158.9
1958	163.1	145.4	166.9	167.3
1959	179.8	158.1	186.1	180.5

Growth in production levels from 1950 (1950 = 100): The statistics show the growth rates. 1950 is the baseline, figures over 100 indicate an increase and below 100 a decline.

Below are a series of definitions listing common reasons why sources are unreliable, and a series of sources. Under each source, explain why the source is either reliable or unreliable for the purpose stated, justifying your answer by referring to the following definitions.

- **Vested interest**: the source is written so that the writer can protect their power or financial interests.
- **Second-hand report**: the writer of the source is not an eyewitness, but is relying on someone else's account.
- **Expertise**: the source is written on a subject in which the author (for example, a historian) is an expert.
- **Political bias**: the source is written by a politician and it reflects their political views.
- **Reputation**: the source is written to protect the writer's reputation.

SOURCE A

A leading German firm describes its economic progress.

As a consequence of the general growth of the economy there was a rise in demand for parts for motor vehicles and engines as well as for other Bosch products. Altogether our turnover increased by nearly 25 per cent. Foreign and internal trade in household equipment made gratifying progress. The turnover of refrigerators and kitchen equipment has increased steadily and we have begun to market these products abroad.

An extract from Bosch's company report of 1955

> The source is reliable/unreliable as evidence for economic growth because
> _____
> _____
> _____

SOURCE B

A British journalist comments on the reasons for West German economic growth.

The Germans have many advantages. They regard work as their national sport and not football. They do not have to pay for rearmament. On the other hand, they were literally eating out of dustbins in 1945 and 1946. The country was smashed in ruins. They have had this colossal influx of refugees to provide a labour force. You can time their amazing recovery from the currency reform of 1948.

An extract from the *Financial Times*, July 1952

> The source is reliable/unreliable as evidence for economic growth because
> _____
> _____
> _____

SOURCE C

George Marshall explains the reasons for the US providing financial aid to countries.

It is logical that the United States should do whatever it is able to do to assist in the return of normal economic health in the world, without which there can be no political stability and no assured peace. Our policy is directed not against any country or doctrine but against hunger, poverty, desperation, and chaos. Its purpose should be the revival of a working economy in the world so as to permit the emergence of political and social conditions in which free institutions can exist. Such assistance, I am convinced, must not be on a piecemeal basis as various crises develop. Any assistance that this Government may render in the future should provide a cure rather than a mere palliative.

An extract from George Marshall's speech at Harvard University, June 1947

> The source is reliable/unreliable as evidence for economic growth because
> _____
> _____
> _____

Western integration

Economic integration

International organisations were established to prevent Germany from waging war again, and to manage the potential of the German economy. However, they became part of the movement for Western European integration. Adenauer made Germany indispensable to the West, made sure Germany was a member of these organisations and rejected closer relations with the East.

October 1949

West Germany joined the Organisation for European Economic Co-operation (**OEEC**) and received Marshall Aid.

April 1951

Germany joined the European Coal and Steel Community (**ECSC**). This placed Franco-German production under a common authority and started European economic unity. This removed foreign control over West German industry, provided her with equal status as a member state and helped reconciliation with France.

1957

West Germany signed the **Treaty of Rome**, which established the European Economic Community (**EEC**), later the EU. In the same year, West Germany joined **EURATOM** (European Atomic Energy Community), a sign of the increased trust and success of Adenauer's policies.

Political integration

The **Council of Europe** was established in 1948. Adenauer joined and stated, 'We belong to the West, not to Soviet Russia.' He accepted the division of Germany and renounced any independent initiative for Germany, which reassured France.

Military integration

NATO was established in 1949, and West Germany joined in 1955. NATO asked Germany to contribute forces to the Korean War, a sign of growing trust, although this concerned France.

Adenauer achieved German rearmament within Europe through NATO, and NATO forces were placed on German soil. Germany also agreed not to seek reunification by force.

Relations with the Soviet Union

These developments concerned Stalin, and in 1952 he contemplated giving up the GDR for a united neutral Germany. However, Stalin insisted that a democratic and united Germany could not join Western powers, because of his concerns about security.

Adenauer ignored all advances from Russia. He also ignored the 1953 Rising in East Berlin (see page 42). However, he did visit Moscow in 1955 and negotiated the return of former prisoners of war (POWs).

Adenauer did not recognise East Germany as a separate state, and refused to have diplomatic relations with countries that did. This was known as the **Hallstein Doctrine** and was not abandoned until the 1970s.

Was Adenauer's foreign policy a success?

Success

- *Rapprochement* with France.
- Rebuilt Germany's reputation in Western Europe.
- Germany was not an outcast, unlike post-1919.
- The return of POWs from Russia in 1955.
- Joined OEEC, ECSC and EEC and NATO.
- Oversaw the 1957 plebiscite for the reincorporation of the Saar into Germany.
- West Germany was treated as an equal, unlike post-1919.

Failure

- He was never able to reconcile the USSR to German rearmament.
- The remilitarisation of German society and the creation of a German army created fear at home.

Spot the inference

High level answers avoid summarising or paraphrasing the sources, and instead make inferences from the sources. Below are a source and a series of statements. Read the source and decide which of the statements:

- make an inference from the source (I)
- paraphrase the source (P)
- summarise the source (S)
- cannot be justified from the source (X).

SOURCE A

Stalin explains his position on a united Germany to Western powers, his second note to them.

The Soviet Union again suggests to the USA, together with the governments of Great Britain and France, to take up the question of a Peace Treaty with Germany and to discuss the question of the unification of Germany and the formation of an all-German government. The Soviet Union sees no reason to delay the solution to this question. It is precisely now that the question is posed of whether Germany can be reconstituted as a state which is united, independent, peace-loving and belonging to the family of peace-loving peoples of Europe, or whether the division of Germany remains, and with that the related danger of a European war.

Stalin's second note to the Western powers about Germany, April 1952

Statement	I	P	S	X
The Soviet Union put forward suggestions for the reunification of Germany.				
The Soviet Union was concerned about the growing power of West Germany.				
Stalin was concerned that West Germany had been integrated into Western Europe.				
The Soviet Union believed that the German question could be solved and a united Germany integrated into the European family, rather than war developing.				
The Soviet Union wanted Britain, France and the USA to discuss Germany's future.				
The Soviet Union was not sincere in its desire for reunification.				
The Soviet Union was willing to give up the GDR in return for a neutral Germany.				
The Soviet Union wanted Germany to remain divided.				

Develop the detail

Below are a question and a paragraph written in answer to this question. The paragraph contains a limited amount of detail. Annotate the paragraph to add additional detail to the answer.

How successful were Adenauer's attempts to integrate West Germany into European affairs?

Adenauer's attempts at integration were successful. He was able to convince European powers of his peaceful intentions and achieved a good relationship with his Western neighbours through various European organisations, acknowledged in his recovery of lost land. West Germany was at the forefront of many European organisations designed to bring about economic integration and later political organisation. The country became trusted militarily and developed its own forces. However, these achievements were at the expense of better relations with the East, although there were some successes. He would not recognise a divided Germany and gave little support to those Germans cut off from West Germany.

Social changes and Adenauer's decline

Many Germans had co-operated with the Nazis. The government needed to win their support, as democracy did not have widespread approval.

The impact of the war

Cities had been damaged and property lost. Nearly 25 per cent of the population were fatherless and women were forced out of work and back into the home because cheap labour was available from the Eastern zones. Refugees from the East numbered 12–13 million, and along with **Gastarbeiters** (guest workers) they also provided cheap labour.

Adenauer was able to win the support of those who lost their possessions in the war through the 1952 Equalisation of Burdens Act. This introduced tax on property and funds not affected by the war and redistributed to those who had suffered the most.

Affluence

Adenauer created an affluent society and concentrated on 'building up' for the future. However, there was unequal distribution of wealth, and social inequalities resulted.

On the positive side there were housing improvements: 430,000 houses were built by 1952, and 4 million by 1957. Wages had risen 400 per cent between 1949 and 1963, there was a ready availability of consumer goods and many people were travelling widely. Social welfare was available, with pensions and an insurance-based health and welfare system. These improvements ended any Communist appeal and helped to create the image of a 'petty bourgeois' (**Spiessburger**), characteristic of the **FRG**, with his cigar, car and new home in a rebuilt city.

There was little social change. The old **elites** still dominated. However, by the 1960s new tensions emerged as economic growth lessened. There was growing electoral support for right-wing groups at a local level and unrest from the left, which was often led by the young, who had new cultural ideas.

Reintegration of former Nazis

Before the FRG was established, reintegration had occurred and quickly, so that by the late 1940s de-Nazification was meaningless. The government compensated those who had suffered, but exonerated most Germans from their crimes. The need to care for war victims and refugees was balanced against responsibilities to the survivors.

Employing Nazis

Former Nazi civil servants regained their jobs lost during de-Nazification through **Law 131**. As a result, 40–80 per cent of civil servants were ex-Nazis and former Nazis continued working in the **judiciary** and universities. Pensions could be claimed for service to the Nazi state and this succeeded in avoiding alienating them. Even Adenauer employed a former Nazi as his personal adviser. The policies ensured that few felt shame or fear of retribution. However, in 1958 an office to investigate possible war crimes opened.

The *Der Spiegel* affair

Adenauer's decline started with his handling of his decision not to run for President in 1959. His withdrawal damaged his image and reputation. This was reinforced by his failure to intervene over the Berlin Wall.

Der Spiegel criticised the readiness of West German defence forces. The Defence Minister misled the Bundestag with his response. The government tried to silence the magazine, raided its offices and arrested journalists in 1962. It appeared as if the government was silencing the press, and this was seen as reminiscent of a dictatorship. The affair led to Adenauer's resignation.

! Support or challenge?

Below is a question which asks you how far you agree with a specific statement. Using your own knowledge and the information in this section decide whether these statements support or challenge the statement in the question and tick the appropriate box.

'Adenauer's Germany was a continuation of the old Germany.' How far do you agree with this view?

	SUPPORT	CHALLENGE
Many old Nazis retained their jobs in the civil service, judiciary and universities.		
Economic policies saw a free market approach.		
Anti-democratic parties were banned to prevent them wrecking democracy.		
The *Der Spiegel* affair showed that the government was still authoritarian.		
Women were forced back into the home, having to give up jobs.		
Adenauer pursued a policy of integration not retribution towards former Nazis.		
West Germany was integrated into Europe economically, politically and militarily.		
The powers of the President were largely formal and symbolic, preventing rule by decree.		

! Explain the difference

The following sources give different accounts of the way former Nazis were to be treated. List the ways in which the sources differ. Explain the differences between the sources using the provenance of the sources alone.

SOURCE A

The ACC directive of 1946 for the removal of former Nazis.

The Tripartite Conference of Berlin included among the purposes of the occupation of Germany: the removal from public and semi-public office and from positions of responsibility in important private undertakings of all members of the Nazi Party who have been more than nominal participants in its activities, and all other persons hostile to Allied purposes. Such persons shall be replaced by persons who, by their political and moral qualities, are deemed capable of assisting in developing genuine democratic institutions in Germany.

Extracts from Control Council Directive No. 24: Removal from office and from positions of responsibility of Nazis and of persons hostile to Allied purposes

SOURCE B

Guidelines issued by the Federal Government.

I. The Federal Government is requested to impress upon the Länder that they should bring to an end the process of de-Nazification, through agreed regulations at Land level, in the light of the following considerations: The restrictions on freedom for all groups (categories) will be lifted.

Limitations on the exercise of a profession or employment will be lifted.

Limitations on active and passive voting rights are lifted.

II. The ending of de-Nazification shall bring to a conclusion the period in which whole groups of people were schematically evaluated with respect to their membership of organisations or institutions of the National-Socialist regime. However, … National-Socialist activists who are guilty under criminal law must be brought to account effectively.

An extract from the Guidelines of the Federal Parliament, issued in December 1950

Exam focus

On pages 67–8 is a sample A-grade answer to the exam-style question below. Read the answer and the examiner comments around it. You could try answering the question below first before looking at the sample answer.

Use your own knowledge to assess how far the sources support the interpretation that the main reason for political stability in West Germany was the political skill of Adenauer.

SOURCE A

Adenauer outlines his policy about restitution and reparations to the survivors of Nazi brutality.

The government and with it the great majority of the German people are aware of the immeasurable suffering that was brought upon the Jews in Germany. The vast majority of the German people rejected the crimes that were committed and did not participate in them. However, unspeakable crimes were committed in the name of the German people, which makes it our duty to make moral and material compensation. In light of the extent of compensation we have to bear in mind the limits to German capacity to deliver that are set by the bitter necessity of looking after the innumerable victims of war and the need to care for refugees and expellees.

An extract from Adenauer's speech to the Bundestag, September 1951

SOURCE B

An American magazine associates Adenauer's popularity with economic recovery.

Firm in his faith, Roman Catholic Adenauer has led his conquered nation back into the society of free nations. This is his greatest claim on the German electorate. Prosperity has been a big factor in his popularity and in the acceptance of democracy. Eight years after the disaster of 1945, the Western half of Germany is rapidly becoming the most powerful nation in Europe. US aid got the wheels of industry turning; German hard work turned revival into boom.

An extract from *Time* magazine, just before the elections of 1953

SOURCE C

A CDU election poster from 1957.

Keine Experimente!
Konrad Adenauer CSU

SOURCE D

A contemporary comment on the reasons for the development of 'Chancellor Democracy'.

From the very outset, opposition of principle against the existing constitutional system and the power of the bureaucratic and especially the military officeholders narrowed down the significance of electoral competition as a political basis for the determination of policy. There was little room left for the development of a concept of legal opposition resting on alternative policy choices propounded by parties working within the constitutional framework.

Otto Kirchheimer, a political scientist, *Germany: the Vanishing Opposition*, written in 1966

SOURCE E

A historian explains the political stability in post-War Germany.

The vast majority of Germans were satisfied with the West German constitution in a way that was never true of the **Weimar** Republic. The Nazis were discredited and the Communists gained less support because of the dislike of East Germany. The army was firmly under civilian control. Lastly, the Republic was consistently prosperous and there was little unemployment in the 1950s. There was no test of democratic institutions such as there was in the Great Depression.

Stewart Easton, *World History Since 1945*, published in 1968

Use your own knowledge to assess how far the sources support the interpretation that the main reason for political stability in West Germany was the political skill of Adenauer.

Sources A and C clearly support the view that political stability in West Germany was due to the political skill of Adenauer; Source B also suggests that economic prosperity, due in part to Adenauer and in part to the hard work of the German people, aided stability. However, Sources D and E place greater emphasis on other political developments, particularly the impact of the constitution and the lack of other parties. And Source E, like Source B, also suggests that economic prosperity was crucial in bringing about stability.

Sources A and C suggest that Adenauer was a skilful politician who clearly understood the mood of the German people and knew how to respond to their concerns. According to Source A, Adenauer provided clear leadership in addressing the controversial issue of war guilt and resolved the difficulties for the German nation, both in terms of the reputation of Germany, but also morally by taking responsibility for compensation. In doing this, he helped to reintegrate Germany into the community of nations, unlike at the end of the First World War, gaining trust abroad. He was also able to win widespread support within Germany as the speech exonerated the vast majority who 'rejected the crimes' and placed a limit on the compensation that could be paid because of looking after the German victims of war; a careful balancing act that won him support. Adenauer was unwilling to risk radical policies and this is also reflected in Source C, where the election poster promises 'No experiment'. This poster reflected the wishes of the people as he won the 1957 election with a majority, gaining over 50 per cent of the vote — the only time a party in West Germany has achieved this — and further supporting the view in Source A that he understood the nation. Not only did a significant number of voters believe this was the best policy, but in 1959 the SPD also recognised the need to abandon radical policies and adopted the Bad Godesberg programme which renounced Marxism and accepted the idea of a state-regulated capitalist democracy, which closely resembled the approach of Adenauer and his CDU. Although both Sources A and C are propaganda, designed to win support by appealing to the people with popular policies and an unwillingness to jeopardise the successes, the results of the elections from 1949 to 1961 suggest that many Germans believed and trusted him and were therefore willing to support him, which helped to bring about stability, suggesting that they are reliable in explaining his political skills and their contribution to stability.

Source B also supports this view to a large extent. It suggests that his success in reintegrating Germany into Europe 'was his greatest claim on the German electorate', seen in joining both the ECSC and NATO and that 'prosperity has been a big factor in his popularity'. This supports the suggestions in Sources A and C that Adenauer understood the German people and was able to deliver policies that satisfied them and, as suggested in Source C, would not see the progress jeopardised. However, the source also suggests that it was not just Adenauer who was responsible for the 'economic miracle' that helped to win him support, as suggested in A, but that US aid played a role as well. However, even this

An excellent introduction; it is source-led and the candidate establishes a sensible grouping of the sources, which should be followed throughout the answer. The candidate is aware that Source B both supports and challenges the view about Adenauer's political skills.

The grouping established in the introduction is continued.

The candidate uses only brief quotations from the sources, but they are relevant to the argument.

The candidate cross-references between Sources C and A.

Precise use of own knowledge to support the argument.

The last sentence links the evaluation back to the question.

Cross-references Source B to A and C.

Uses own knowledge and historical debate to evaluate the role of the US.

Last sentence of the paragraph links back to the question set and makes a judgement.

Deals with the sources as a pair.

Evaluates using own knowledge of the Basic Law and constitutional restraints.

Good cross referencing between a range of sources.

Clear judgement reached, which has been supported and refers back to the sources.

qualification does not go far enough, as many historians believe that it was the currency reform and the policies of Erhard that revived the economy and helped to create the long-term stability. Although the source appears to give a balanced view about the reasons for stability, it was written in 1953 and considers only part of the period, and as an American magazine might overemphasise its own nation's role, but it does acknowledge that Adenauer's political skills were important.

Sources D and E put forward other reasons for political stability. Both argue that a lack of political opposition helped to create stability. Source D suggests that there was little room for the development of legal opposition and Source E argues that alternatives, such as the Nazis or Communists, had been discredited. These developments, along with the constitution, which according to Source E was also popular, limited political opposition and helped to ensure that a multi-party system gradually withered away, resulting in elections becoming little more than plebiscites on Adenauer. This argument has some justification as the SRP and KPD were both banned and the '5 per cent hurdle' also made it difficult for smaller parties. However, Source E also agrees in part with Source B about the importance of economic prosperity, but unlike B it does not credit Adenauer with that success, but it did mean that democratic institutions were never challenged as they were under Weimar. Both sources are written by authorities in their area, although the author of D, a political scientist, may have particular views about the concept of 'Chancellor Democracy', which has influenced his arguments, but the historian in E offers a range of reasons for stability and is supported by the election results and economic statistics.

Adenauer's role and political skills were certainly important in bringing about stability, as shown in Sources A and C. However, other factors such as the economic miracle and other political developments, particularly the Basic Law, contributed. How far Adenauer's skills brought about the economic miracle is open to debate, but he did at least uphold the conditions in which it was possible and provided the peaceful integration with the West that allowed it to flourish, so that West Germany did not face the same problems as the Weimar, supporting the view that his political skills were crucial.

64/70

This is a very good answer that uses all the sources to reach a balanced judgement that has been sustained throughout the answer. The understanding of the sources is excellent, although to gain full marks more could have been said about Source D. Own knowledge is integrated into the answer and used very well to support the sources and to aid their evaluation. The knowledge is well selected and always relevant to the point under discussion. The candidate is certainly aware of how the factors are linked and how Adenauer understood and responded to the public mood, at least until the end of his period in office.

What makes a good answer?

List the characteristics of a good answer to a part (b) question (see page 2), using the example and examiner comments above.

Rewrite the paragraph

Using the comments above, rewrite paragraph four so that there is more use of Source D.

Glossary

Affidavit A written statement that is confirmed on oath.

Anti-feminist ideology A set of beliefs that women are inferior to men and play a subordinate role in society.

Anti-Semitism A hostility or dislike of Jews.

Aryan Nordic or Anglo-Saxon races that the Nazis believed were superior.

Asocials A term used to describe various groups of people who the Nazis believed were damaging to society.

Auxiliaries Those who provide additional support for full-time members of the armed forces.

Basic Law The constitution of West Germany established in 1949. It was to be temporary until there was a united Germany.

Berlin Wall Wall constructed in August 1961 by the Communist powers to cut off East Berlin from the West. It was erected to prevent workers leaving the East as it was their last escape route.

Bezirke Small local units which replaced the five regions in East Germany in 1952.

Bizonia The name used to describe the merged military zones of Britain and the USA.

Black market Illegal trade in scarce goods.

Bomb Plot This plot attempted to assassinate Hitler on 20 July 1944. It involved both civilian resistance figures and army officers, including Colonel von Stauffenberg. He placed a bomb in a meeting room, but its movement before the meeting probably saved Hitler's life and in the confusion afterwards supporters of Hitler were able to arrest the conspirators.

Bormann Martin Bormann's first major job was to organise the Nazi Party, but in 1943 he became Hitler's secretary.

Boycott Refusing to deal with someone or something, in this case refusing to shop in Jewish shops.

Bundesrat The Upper House of the West German parliament; it looked after the interests of the states.

Bundestag The Lower House of the West German parliament.

Cabinet The group of senior ministers who drew up government policy.

Capitalism A system in which industry and trade are controlled by private ownership.

Catholic Youth Catholic youth group which was independent of Nazi control.

Chancellor The head of government.

Chancellor Democracy Term used to describe the government of Adenauer, where it was argued competitive elections had been replaced by plebiscites in favour of the government.

Coalition A government formed from the support of two or more parties in order to achieve a majority.

Collectivisation The combination of small independent farms into a larger farm under state control.

Concordat An agreement between Church and state.

Council of Europe An early forerunner of the EEC, but lacked power.

Cult of personality Using charisma and other personal qualities as a political leader to dominate the state.

DAF The German Labour Front, established by the Nazis in 1933 to replace independent trade unions. It helped to control the workers.

Democratic centralism Decisions taken at the centre are passed down to the people. Views of the people should be influenced by the Communist Party and passed up to the centre.

De-Stalinisation The policy followed by the Russian leader Nikita Khrushchev. He denounced Stalin's policies as tyrannical at a meeting of the Communist International in 1956, which he gave to those in Eastern Europe of greater freedom.

Dualism A system of government in which two political forces appear to govern the country; in this instance, the Nazi Party and the state.

ECSC The European Coal and Steel Community, established to co-ordinate steel and coal production.

EEC The forerunner of the EU, established in 1957 and consisting of six member nations. Initially it was a customs union allowing free movement of goods, capital and labour.

Einsatzgruppen SS units responsible for rounding up and murdering Jews in Eastern Europe.

Elites Term used to describe the conservative groups within German society who dominated the army, judiciary and civil service.

Enabling Act The legal transfer of power to the Cabinet in Germany; it effectively gave Hitler full powers and created the dictatorship.

Ethnic Germans Pure-born Germans who shared a common culture.

EURATOM Set up to co-ordinate the development of nuclear energy in Western Europe.

Euthanasia The killing of those too ill, old or handicapped to work.

Fatherland A person's native country, but usually associated with a patriotic feeling towards it.

Final Solution The term used by the Nazis to describe the extermination of the Jews, begun in 1941.

First past the post An electoral system where the candidate who wins the most votes, not necessarily a majority, is elected.

Five Year Plans State plans and targets for economic development to be met in a five-year period.

Four Year Plan A plan for the economy established by Goering in 1936; the aim was to increase re-armament and make Germany self-sufficient.

FRG The Federal Republic of Germany, or West Germany.

Führerprinzip Leadership principle, a one-party state with an all-powerful leader.

Gastarbeiter Overseas workers or guest workers, often from south-east Europe, who worked in West Germany, often for low rates of pay; they had no political rights.

Gauleiters A Nazi official responsible for the administration of a province.

GDR The German Democratic Republic, or East Germany.

Genocide The organised murder of an ethic group.

Gestapo The secret police.

Ghettoes The area in a city inhabited by Jews; under Nazi rule they were separated from other citizens and lived in overcrowded conditions.

Gleischaltung The co-ordination or bringing into line of people so that they act in the same way.

Grammar schools Selective schools that followed a more academic curriculum than other Nazi schools.

Hallstein Doctrine West Germany would not formally recognise East Germany.

Herrenvolk The racially dominant people who govern.

Hitler Youth The name for the range of youth groups under Nazi control. By 1939 membership was compulsory.

Horst Wessel Nazi Stormtrooper killed in a fight with Communists. The song he had written became a Nazi marching song.

Hungarian Uprising Uprising in 1956 which saw the Hungarian leader, Nagy, draw up plans for free elections and to leave the Warsaw Pact. Russian troops were sent in and there were two weeks of fighting before it was crushed. Nagy was executed.

Ideology A system of beliefs.

Indoctrinate The teaching of a particular view so that it will be accepted and other views rejected.

Judiciary The system of courts in which judges administer justice.

Junkers Landowning and aristocratic families, usually associated with the eastern areas of Germany.

Karl Marx Marx was a nineteenth-century political thinker who provided the theoretical basis for communism. He argued that economic factors determined the course of history and that ultimately the workers would unite and throw off capitalism so that they were not exploited.

Khrushchev The leader of the Soviet Union after Stalin.

Korean War War between North and South Korea which lasted from 1950 to 1953. United Nations troops aided the South, while China aided the North.

Kripo The criminal police within the Nazi state. They were often plain-clothed detectives who were concerned with serious crimes. They had offices in major towns and cities. They were under the control of the SS and were merged with the Gestapo.

Kristallnacht Known as the 'Night of Broken Glass', it occurred on 9–10 November 1938. It saw the destruction of large numbers of Jewish businesses, shops and synagogues. The Nazis claimed it was in response to the assassination of the German ambassador in Paris by a Jew.

Labour exchanges Local offices set up by the state where the unemployed went to find jobs.

Länder The parliaments of the German states.

Länderkammer Upper House in the East German parliament, represented the five regions.

Law 131 A law introduced in 1951 as part of the German constitution which gave former Nazi civil servants the right to reinstatement in their former jobs.

Lebensraum 'Living space' territory in which Germany wanted to be able to maintain the German race.

London Conference Conference of Western powers from February to June 1948 that agreed on a currency and the formation of the state of West Germany.

Marshall Aid/Plan The plan proposed by the US General George Marshall to give financial aid to nations in Europe to help them rebuild their economies and to stop the spread of communism.

Marxist-Leninist A combination of beliefs in Marx's commitment to overthrow capitalism and Lenin's idea of the role of the party.

NATO North Atlantic Treaty Organisation, a military agreement between many Western European states.

New Course The plan to change the direction of Soviet policy after the death of Stalin in 1953.

New Order The term used to describe the economic, political and social integration of Europe under Nazi rule.

Oder-Neisse line The border between East Germany and Poland, so called because of the two rivers that formed the boundary.

OEEC Organisation for European Economic Co-operation, made up of Western nations; they received Marshall Aid. The aim was to rebuild the Western European economy.

Parliamentary Council This was established in 1948 and was the forerunner of the West German Lower Chamber in parliament. Its role was to draw up a constitution, the Basic Law, for West Germany and was then dissolved.

Pastor Niemöller Although he had sympathised with Nazi views in the 1920s, he turned against them because of their anti-Semitism and helped to form the Confessional Church. He was arrested in 1937 after a sermon criticising the government and was imprisoned until the end of the war.

Patriotism A love of one's country.

People's Community The ideal Nazi community made up of pure Germans or Aryans.

Plebiscite A vote by the people to decide a specific issue, similar to a referendum. A vote was held in 1935 to decide the future of the Saar, as had been agreed in the Treaty of Versailles.

Politburo The main executive body of Soviet government, responsible for defining and putting into practice government policy.

President The elected head of a republic.

Propaganda Information spread by political groups which is often exaggerated or biased.

Proportional representation A voting system where each party is represented in parliament in proportion to the number of votes they receive.

Putsch A violent rising or attempted seizure of power.

Racial genetics The belief that a person's race determined their genetic make-up and therefore their behaviour.

Reichstag The parliament of Germany under the Reich, created in 1871.

Reparations Payments made by a defeated nation to compensate for the damage caused.

RSHA The Reich Security Office. This brought together all the police and security organisations.

Ruhr An important industrial area of Germany, which produced large amounts of steel.

SA The Brown Shirts, so called because of the colour of their uniform. They were known as the Stormtroopers and were established in 1921 under the leadership of Ernst Röhm.

Saar An area in Germany rich in coal and iron ore.

SD The intelligence branch of the SS.

Seven Year Plan Economic plan introduced in East Germany, giving greater flexibility and reintroducing the idea of profit.

Social Darwinism Belief that life is a competition and that the fittest deserve to prosper whilst the unfit deserve to be left behind.

Social justice A fair distribution of wealth, income and social equality and status.

Spiessburger In West Germany a member of the 'petty bourgeois' who had gained from the improved standards of living created by the economic miracle.

SS Established in 1925 as Hitler's bodyguard, during the 1930s and 1940s they became the Nazi elite. They were led by Himmler.

'Stab in the back' myth The view that the German army had not lost the First World War, but been betrayed by forces at home such as Socialists and Jews. This weakened the Weimar government.

Stalinist Supporter of Stalin's beliefs in centralisation, state control and his views of communism.

Stasi The East German secret police.

Strasser Gregor Strasser led the North German Nazis in the 1920s and was the leading supporter of the socialist and anti-capitalist element of the Nazi Party.

Teutonic paganism Non-Christian beliefs of Germans from the past.

Totalitarian A system of government where all power is centralised and there are no rival authorities.

Treaty of Rome The treaty that established the European Economic Community, the forerunner of the EU.

Treaty of Versailles The treaty at end of the First World War. This declared Germany guilty of starting the war and caused much resentment within Germany that Hitler was able to exploit.

Trizonia The term used to describe the unification of the three Western zones of Germany after the war; France joined Bizonia.

Truman Doctrine US foreign policy aim to support governments fighting for 'freedom' against communism.

Unreliables Nazi term for those whose support for Nazism and its beliefs could not be trusted.

Untermenschen 'Racially inferior' people.

Volk A 'people' who have the same ethnic identity.

Volkisch A German term used to describe a policy based on the concept of race, to protect the superior German race from inferior races.

Volkseigene Betriebe 'People's Own Factory' but owned and managed by the state.

Volksgemeinschaft A people's community, a socially and racially united community.

Volkskammer East German parliament.

Waffen SS Racially pure and fanatical units of the SS involved in the advances into Eastern Europe.

Wannsee Conference held in 1942 at which the Final Solution of the Jewish question in Europe was agreed.

Weimar A town outside Berlin where the government of Germany met after the First World War because Berlin was too dangerous. The town gave its name to the Republic that was established after the War.

Welfare state A state system that protects the health and well-being of all of its citizens, particularly those in need.

Workshy Nazi term to describe those who they believed could work and contribute to the *Volk*, but would not work.

Timeline

1933 January: Hitler appointed Chancellor

February: Reichstag fire

March: Elections

Enabling Act

Establishment of concentration camps, originally for political prisoners

April: Boycott of Jewish businesses

July: One-party state established

Concordat signed with Papacy

Sterilisation Law

1934 Confessional Church established to resist Nazi control of Protestant Churches

Night of the Long Knives removed the SA from influence

Death of Hindenburg; Hitler combines office of Chancellor and President; Army swear oath of loyalty to Hitler

1935 Nuremberg Race Laws

Establishment of Ministry of Church Affairs to co-ordinate Churches

Introduction of *Lebensborn* to improve racial quality

Mass arrests of Socialists and Communists by Gestapo

1936 Goering introduces Four Year Plan to help preparations for war

1937 Nazi relaxation of policy towards women because they need workers

1938 Decree for the 'Struggle against the Gypsy Plague'

Kristallnacht: attacks on Jewish property and synagogues

1939 Made compulsory to join the Hitler Youth

Euthanasia campaign started

1941 Bishop Galen's sermon against euthanasia

1942 Wannsee Conference, agrees on the Final Solution for the Jewish problem

1944 Stauffenberg Bomb Plot

Execution of Edelweiss Pirates in Cologne

1945 February: Yalta Conference

April: death of Hitler

May: surrender of Germany

July–August: Potsdam Conference

1946 Formation of Socialist Unity Party in Eastern zone of Germany following merger of KPD and SPD

Law for the Democratisation of German Schools removes RE from East German education system

1947 Formation of Bizonia following merger of US and British zones

Truman Doctrine announced by US President offering support to nations fighting communism

Marshall Plan offers aid to Europe

1948 Currency reform in Western zones, followed by reform in Eastern zone

Berlin Blockade starts

Western representatives meet and discuss constitution for new democratic Western German state

1949 Formation of Trizonia as France joins Bizonia

Berlin Blockade ends

May: West Germany (Federal Republic) comes into existence

August: Adenauer elected Chancellor of West Germany

West Germany joins Organisation for European Economic Co-operation (OEEC)

October: East Germany (Democratic Republic) comes into existence

1950 Creation of Stasi in East Germany

Outbreak of Korean War

1951 West Germany joins European Coal and Steel Community (ECSC)

1952 First series of collectivisation in East Germany

SRP outlawed in West Germany

Stalin's notes suggesting unification of Germany

1953 Death of Stalin

Berlin Rising

Five per cent hurdle introduced for elections in West Germany

Adenauer wins second election

1954 Youth Dedication Service reintroduced and imposed in East Germany

1955 West Germany joins NATO

Warsaw Pact established as a response to NATO

Adenauer visits Moscow and secures return of former POWs

Recreation of West German army

1956 KPD outlawed in West Germany

Hungarian Uprising

1957 Adenauer wins third election with overall majority

Establishment of European Economic Community (EEC)

Saar plebiscite, returns it to West Germany

CDU renounce Ahlen Programme

West Germany joins EURATOM

1959 Bad Godesberg Programme adopted by SPD in West Germany

1960 Second wave of collectivisation in East Germany

1961 Building of Berlin Wall

Adenauer wins fourth victory but reduction in number of seats

1962 *Der Spiegel* affair

1963 Resignation of Adenauer

New Economic System for Planning and Direction introduced in East Germany

Answers

Section 1: How effectively did Hitler establish and consolidate Nazi authority 1933–45?

Page 5, Spot the inference

Goebbels and the Nazis had been converted to supporters of democracy. (X)

The Nazis were willing to use democracy to help them gain power. (I)

Having been elected to the Reichstag, the Nazis will use the democratic system to destroy democracy. (S)

Like Mussolini, the Nazis would use all the elements of democracy to help them gain power and then tear it apart. (P)

The Nazis believed that democracy would destroy itself. The Nazis did not believe in democracy. (I)

Weimar democracy was strong; that is why the Nazis wanted its weapons. (X)

The Nazis intended to use legal means to overthrow democracy. (S)

Page 7, Support or challenge?

Hitler's appointment as Chancellor was the result of constitutional procedures. **Challenge**

Nazi support was in decline and therefore they had to seize power. **Support**

It was electoral support that brought Hitler to power. **Challenge**

Intrigue, rather than seizure of power, best describes Hitler's appointment as Chancellor. **Challenge**

Rather than seizing power, other figures believed they were using Hitler. **Challenge**

The events of January 1933 have only been called a seizure of power by the press. **Challenge**

It appealed to Hitler's sense of drama that the events of January 1933 were called a seizure of power. **Challenge**

Hitler's dislike of democracy resulted in the events of January 1933 being called a seizure of power. **Challenge**

Hitler and the Nazi Party came to power because of their electoral strength. **Challenge**

Page 9, Explain the difference: suggested answer

Source A's account, based on Ernst's testimony, argues that the latter led members of the SA into the Reichstag through a secret passage and once in the building, they started the fire. However, Source B records Hitler's immediate reaction to the fire, in which he implies it is the start of the Communist rising.

Hitler wanted a reason to attack the Communists as they were his main political threat and blaming them for the fire would provide the opportunity to bring in legislation attacking the Communist Party. He therefore had reasons to manipulate events, whereas Shirer's account is based on the testimony of Ernst who was there. As Ernst was purged the following year it may have been because he knew the exact events, which the Nazi Party wanted to suppress.

Page 9, Write the question: suggested answer

Compare the sources as evidence for support for a second revolution in Germany.

OR

Compare the sources as evidence of instability and division within Germany in 1933.

Page 13, Spot the inference

The SPD were less successful than the Communists in maintaining support. (X)

The Communists gained much support among the working class. (X)

There was a significant amount of opposition to the Nazi regime. (I)

The Gestapo found it increasingly difficult to monitor the activities of opponents. (S)

Opposition was well organised. (I)

The Communists' and Socialists' propaganda was still spread effectively in factories and other clubs. (P)

The Gestapo was able to successfully prosecute opponents due to the availability of evidence. (X)

The Nazi regime was weakened by the scale of opposition. (X)

Page 15, Support or challenge?

Source A. **Support**

Source B. **Challenge**

Source C. **Challenge**

Source D. **Support**

Source E. **Support**

Gestapo numbers were limited and this made opposition much easier. **Challenge**

Opposition lacked organisation and this made it weak. **Support**

Most people simply accepted the regime and were happy that they had work. **Support**

Opposition groups continued to exist throughout the period. **Challenge**

Pamphlets that opposition groups produced had little impact. **Support**

People were too frightened to listen to messages of opposition. **Support**

There were a large number of different opposition groups. **Challenge**

Page 15, Doing reliability well

Source A: It could be seen as unreliable as evidence for opposition because of the vested interest of Nazis to show efficiency and to protect their reputation of being efficient. However, it admits Nazis are not able to control all opposition and this suggests it might be reliable.

Source B: Although written by the Gestapo, they did have expertise about the actions of political parties and in admitting the successes of the Communists it is likely to be reliable in offering information about opposition.

Source C: It could be unreliable as evidence about opposition as it reflects the writer's political views about the need to resist the Nazis. It also reflects the author's vested interest to show they did take action to protect his standing.

Source D: Although it might be unreliable as evidence because the writer has a vested interest to explain why he did not resist Nazism so wants to protect his reputation and not appear pro-Nazi, he is a historian and therefore an expert who has no reason to avoid recalling the truth.

Source E: Although it might be unreliable as evidence for opposition because of its political bias (it was written by a member of the conservative opposition and shows conservative resistance), it comes from a private diary so it is more likely to be reliable, particularly as it admits the limits of their effectiveness.

Section 2: To what extent did the Nazis transform German society?

Page 21, Support or challenge?

There was a great deal of emphasis on PE in the Nazi curriculum. **Support**

Girls were taught the importance of being healthy. **Challenge**

Racial studies formed a key part of the Nazi curriculum. **Challenge**

In the Hitler Youth, much time was devoted to marching, camping and hiking. **Support**

History lessons were largely about German history from the First World War. **Challenge**

Nazi ideology was taught in both schools and in the Hitler Youth. **Challenge**

Maths lessons were often based around the angles of missiles and projectiles or the bombing of Jewish ghettoes. **Support**

Page 21, Write the question: suggested answer

Compare the sources as evidence that the youth of Germany enjoyed the activities of the Hitler Youth.

OR

Compare the sources as evidence for the success of the Hitler Youth in indoctrinating the young in Germany.

Page 25, Explain the difference: suggested answer

Source A suggests that the Churches were struggling and that there was a decline in support for religion because of the pressure of the Nazi regime. However, Sources B and C both stress the successful impact of the Churches; Source B argues that more are going to church, although it admits not the young, whilst Source C suggests that the Church is undermining the Nazi regime.

Source A is written by a teacher who the locals want removed and this probably explains why she thinks the Nazis are grinding the local population down, whereas Source B, a local church report, may only reflect the situation in that area, but would also want to encourage the Church. Source C was written during the war when support for the Church grew as people looked for consolation, but the Nazis would see it as undermining their position.

Page 27, Doing reliability well: suggested answer

Source A: It is likely to be reliable as an indicator of the response of ordinary Germans. Gibbs was an eyewitness reporter and an expert journalist who would be aware of what to observe and the conclusions that can be drawn. He had no need to distort the truth for his audience.

Source B: It was in the vested interest of the party and the report to argue the rally was a success, suggesting the source is unreliable. However, those taking part in the rally are leading members of the Nazi organisation and so they are bound to support it and this response is corroborated by Riefenstahl's film.

Page 29, Spot the inference

Nazi racial policy was a success. (X)

The Nazis wanted to introduce a policy of selective breeding similar to that used in farming. (S)

Nazi racial policy aimed to purify the German nation. (I)

Nazism had no place for weakness and wanted to remove it from German society. (I)

Only the pure-blooded would be allowed to breed so as to remove weaker elements. (S)

The Nazis wanted only pure-bred Germans as part of the nation. (P)

Page 33, Doing reliability well

Source C: Goebbels, as Minister of Propaganda, has a vested interest in showing that Nazi policies are popular and therefore this description of feelings is likely to be unreliable. He may also have a political bias in arguing that policies are popular.

Source D: It is a second-hand report from exile so may not have full knowledge and therefore be unreliable. However, the report is balanced, showing successes and failures, which might not be expected from an opposition group so there may be elements of reliability.

Source E: The vested interest of Funk to protect himself at the war trial and move the blame to others makes the source unreliable.

Section 3: To what extent and in what ways did communism transform the GDR?

Page 39, Spot the inference

There was a determination to punish former Nazis by taking away their economic power. (S)

The Communists wanted to appear democratic. (I)

The industrial activities of former Nazis have been put at the disposal of the new administration. (P)

It was the Nazis who plunged Europe into war and they should be punished. (P)

Democratic practices were already in place in Saxony. (X)

The Soviet forces appeared to be reasonable by allowing a referendum. (I)

The Soviets wanted to win popular support through their policies. (I)

There was much former Nazi property to be disposed of. (X)

Page 41, Support or challenge?

Elections were to be held in Germany, starting at local level. **Challenge**

A range of political parties were established in the Russian zone. **Challenge**

Communists were to be in charge of Personnel Questions and Education. **Support**

Not all mayors were Communists. **Challenge**

All parties were brought together in a 'National Front'. **Challenge**

Mass organisations were put under Communist control. **Support**

Liberal and religious parties were allowed. **Challenge**

Source A. **Support**

Source B. **Challenge**

Page 43, Doing reliability well

Source A: This is unreliable as evidence for the causes of unrest because of political bias. It was produced by the East German government who would want to blame outside forces and detract from the unpopularity of their own policies. As it was for external consumption they would not admit their own failings.

Source B: Although it might be expected that an SED report about the causes of unrest would be unreliable, this is likely to be reliable because it is an internal report which would want to identify the real causes to prevent a recurrence. As it was for internal party consumption, it would be free from any political bias.

Page 47, Explain the difference: suggested answer

The refugee in Source A must have found conditions bad to have fled and may therefore exaggerate to explain his decision. The woman in Source B had suffered terribly in the earlier period; now life appeared to be better and therefore she would be pleased with the state.

Page 47, Develop the detail: suggested answer

The advent of Communist rule brought about increased opportunities for many groups in East German society, **such as peasants and factory workers**, who supported Communist rule. Loyal workers had increased social and economic opportunities, **such as better education and management opportunities and better machinery** and women were also able to play an increased role in society due to social provisions **such as improved maternity care, crèches and after-**

school facilities. The same was true of children from working class backgrounds as educational opportunities, **such as scholarships and university opportunities** were provided for them. However, these gains must be balanced against the control the party had over individuals through mass organisations, **such as the Democratic Women's League of Germany or the Society for Sport and Technology** which controlled a wide range of aspects of life.

Page 49, Explain the difference: suggested answer

The first account by the US (Source A) is an attempt to counter the Soviet view and persuade them that the East Germans have admitted there are internal problems, whereas Ulbricht (Source B) is trying to justify his government's response to British MPs.

Page 49, Doing reliability well

Source A: The writer is an expert; he lived in the West and was involved in buying cheap goods from the East, making him more likely to be reliable. However, it might be argued there was some political bias as the person is from the West and would want to show how much better the West was, hence the complaint about being caught with low-priced goods on the way back into West Berlin. The cost of living in the West was higher, suggesting there was a better standard of living. Wages were lower in the East which meant prices were lower too so people could afford the goods.

Source B: Written by the East German government to justify their actions in closing the border it is likely to have political bias and therefore be unreliable. The East Germans would also want to defend their reputation and defend their actions and not admit that there are problems within their area, but argue the problems are due to the West, again making the account unreliable.

Source C: Although Adenauer does not directly comment on the causes, his account is likely to be politically biased because he was Chancellor in the West and wanted to show sympathy with those in the East for political gain and to criticise the East.

Section 4: How far did Western democratic structures succeed in the Federal Republic?

Page 55, Support or challenge?

There were severe food and fuel shortages in the Western zone. **Support**

There had been a large influx of refugees from the East. **Challenge**

The Western zone had suffered large-scale damage during the war. **Support**

The new government had to overcome the impact of Nazi rule and genocide. **Challenge**

The structure of the ACC and the need to achieve unanimous decisions created difficulties. **Challenge**

There were divisions between France, USA and Great Britain. **Challenge**

The weakness of the British economy meant they were unable to support their zone. **Support**

The weakness of the German currency and the resultant black market created economic problems. **Support**

Inflation severely damaged the economy in the Western zone. **Support**

Page 55, Spot the inference

Conditions within Germany were bad. (P)

Russia was the main obstacle to German recovery. (X)

The USA wanted to unite Germany. (I)

The USA wanted greater economic unity. (S)

The USA wanted Germany to be able to recover economically. (P)

Economic prosperity was needed for German recovery. (S)

There were tensions among the wartime Allies. (I)

Economic barriers were hindering Germany reaching the targets agreed. (S)

Page 57, Develop the detail: suggested answer

There were many elements of the Basic Law, **such as combining PR with first past the post and an agreement all parties had upheld democracy, and the indirect election of the President thus ensuring he was a supporter of democracy,** that were designed to prevent a repeat of 1932–3. Political parties had to support the system and those that did not, **such as the KPD and SRP**, were banned. The President was not voted for by the people **but elected indirectly** and his powers were limited. The Chancellor had to be approved by parliament and could not be simply dismissed by the President. The voting system was designed to prevent small parties from being represented, **they had to gain 5 per cent of the vote**, and the combination of two electoral systems **of PR and first past the post** also ensured that more extreme parties were unlikely to gain seats.

Page 59, Explain the difference: suggested answer

Source A suggests that Adenauer played down the importance of the Wall, shown through his continuation of the election campaign and failure to go to see Brandt and even attacking him, whereas Source B sees the Wall as evidence of weakness in the East and suggests that it should be used as an opportunity to move towards rapprochement, which he hopes will lead to a relaxation of the border and the wall. The difference clearly reflects the attitudes of the two different parties. Adenauer followed a policy of no rapprochement with the East and had clearly thrown his political weight behind the West, whereas Source B, written by a Social Democrat, reflects their desire to improve relations with the East.

Page 61, Doing reliability well: suggested answer

Source A: It might be seen as unreliable because the company had a vested interest in showing how well the company was doing and a reputation to uphold of high quality goods and success. However, it is unlikely that the figures would be inaccurate as the author is an expert.

Source B: The account is likely to be reliable as an explanation for economic growth as it is written by an expert, who was writing for a reputable paper, the *Financial Times*. This means they would have had an understanding of the economy, but would also have had their reputation for honest journalism to uphold.

Source C: This may be less reliable because of political bias to defend the Marshall Plan and to try to deflect the claims it was for political gains. Marshall also had a vested interest in showing the USA in a good light and this may also make him exaggerate the claims.

Page 63, Spot the inference

The Soviet Union put forward suggestions for the reunification of Germany. (S)

The Soviet Union was concerned about the growing power of West Germany. (I)

Stalin was concerned that West Germany had been integrated into Western Europe. (I)

The Soviet Union believed that the German question could be solved and a united Germany integrated into the European family, rather than war developing. (P)

The Soviet Union wanted Britain, France and the USA to discuss Germany's future. (S)

The Soviet Union was not sincere in its desire for reunification. (X)

The Soviet Union was willing to give up the GDR in return for a neutral Germany. (I)

The Soviet Union wanted Germany to remain divided. (X)

Page 63, Develop the detail: suggested answer

Adenauer's attempts at integration were successful. He was able to convince European powers of his peaceful intentions and achieved a good relationship with his Western neighbours, **particularly France**, through various European organisations, **including the OEEC**, acknowledged in his recovery of lost land **with the Saar regained in 1957**. West Germany was at the forefront of many European organisations designed to bring about economic integration **such as the ECSC and the EEC** and later political organisation, **such as the European Council**. The country became trusted militarily joining NATO and developed its own forces. However, these achievements were at the expense of better relations with the East, although there were some successes **with the return of former POWs from Russia in 1957**. He would not recognise a divided Germany, **upholding the Hallstein Doctrine**, and gave little support to those Germans cut off from West Germany.

Page 65, Support or challenge?

Many old Nazis retained their jobs in the civil service, judiciary and universities. **Support**

Economic policies saw a free market approach. **Challenge**

Anti-democratic parties were banned to prevent them wrecking democracy. **Challenge**

The *Der Spiegel* affair showed that the government was still authoritarian. **Support**

Women were forced back into the home, having to give up jobs. **Support**

Adenauer pursued a policy of integration not retribution towards former Nazis. **Support**

West Germany was integrated into Europe economically, politically and militarily. **Challenge**

The powers of the President were largely formal and symbolic, preventing rule by decree. **Challenge**

Page 65, Explain the difference: suggested answer

Source A is from soon after the war when the Allies were in control and there was an unrealistic view that all former Nazis could be dealt with, whereas Source B is from Adenauer's government who wanted reconciliation.

Notes

Notes

Notes